雅思考试攻略

如何做选择题

版权声明

版权© 2018均属 Complete Test Preparation公司所有。

本书所有内容，在未经原作者的允许下，任何人不得以发布或修改成其他的版本，或者以图像，电子，或者其他包括影印，录像，网站，录音或者任何信息储存处理的形式进行转载。违反者将依法追究责任。

注意：Complete Test Preparation公司在本书的内容上做了极大的努力，以此来为考生提供准确，完整，和及时的考试信息和资料。但是，考试内容以考试中出现的为准，考试管理部门有可能随时对试卷上的内容进行修改。Complete Test Preparation公司不能对此行为进行担保或负任何责任，同时也不能保证本书中的内容和真实考卷中的内容在准确性，及时性，或者完整性上完全一致。Complete Test Preparation公司不存在代表，担保，表明或者暗示本教材中任何内容的完整性，准确性，可靠性，实用性或信息的有效性。因此任何对于信息的依赖所产生的后果，将由个人承担。

作者对于使用本书所产生的后果，不论直接还是间接使用，都不负有法律责任。经协定，销售后作者不参与任何专业服务或给出任何指导型建议。如果需要专业的建议或指导，请向专业的部门寻求服务。此次出版中的公司，产品以及服务名称均具有识别目的。所有商标和注册商标均属于企业持有人的财产。Complete Test Preparation公司不隶属于任何教学机构。

ISBN-13: 9781772452594

Version 4.5 May 2018

IELTS® 是美国教育考试服务中心的注册商标，没有参与本书的出版，也与本书的发行没有任何关系。

出版

Complete Test Preparation公司
加拿大不列颠哥伦比亚省维多利亚市

登陆我们的官网 https://www.test-preparation.ca

自2005年以来，Complete Test Preparation公司出版发行过很多高质量的考试辅导教材。每年都有成千上万的学生来访问我们的网站，并有来自全世界不同地区的学生，老师和家长购买我们的教学材料，课程，指导教材和模拟试题。
Complete Test Preparation公司一直致力于在市场中为学生提供最优质的考试教材和雅思练习测试。我们团队的成员都是高学历，并有着多年丰富的教学经验的作者和编辑。

公司位于自加拿大不列颠哥伦比亚省维多利亚市。

反馈

我们乐于收到您的反馈。发送您的想法和建议到feedback@test-preparation.ca。我们会认真考虑您提出的建议并把相关内容补充到升级版本中。

www.facebook.com/CompleteTestPreparation

目录

6 考试总览
    考试策略   8
    什么样的人能答好选择题?   9

10 选择题快速答题技巧
    什么样的人能答好选择题?   13
    回答选择题的具体步骤   14

18 选择题答题策略练习题
    应答键   41

67 阅读理解练习题
    应答键   85

104 听力
    应答键   121

124 如何写作文
    写作中的常见错误 – 示例 1   134
    写作中的常见错误 – 示例 2   136
    言简意赅   139
    避免词句的重复使用   141

148 如何应对口语考试
    准备口语考试   148
    练习   149
    口语考试   150

152 如何备战考试
    学习方法   153
    精神准备 – 如何为考试做好心里准备   154
    阅读题目要求   156
    如何考试 – 基本原则   157

158 与时间交朋友
   在考场中 – 你一定要做的几件事！　161
   考试前避免焦虑　　　　　　　　　166
   常见考试错误　　　　　　　　　　168

171 考试结束后

开启准备工作

恭喜你！当你决定参加雅思考试的时候，你已经向美好的未来迈出了第一步！当然，除非你打算尽最大的努力来争取得到尽可能高的分数，不然是没有必要参加这个重要考试的。也就是说，安排好你的时间，并找到学习材料的最好方法，思路和策略。没错，准备考试会花掉你大量的时间和经历，但是如果你愿意集中精神合理分配时间的话，你在考试中自然而然会发挥出色，取得优异的成绩！我们知道努力完成一件事可能是有点可怕的，因为你不知道应当从哪里开始着手。而这就是我们在这里的原因。这本学习指导可以帮助你提高你的应试能力，通过介绍给你一些技巧来提升你的水平和自信。

雅思考试介绍

考试基本介绍

国际英语测试系统 (IELTS) 是一个被广泛认可的语言能力测试，应试者需要用英语进行学习或生活交流。雅思考试由三个主办方创办，剑桥大学的剑桥英语语言测试中心；英国文化委员会以及IDP教育集团（通过其子公司雅思澳大利亚有限公司执行）。雅思为笔试考试。登录官方网站可以查找更多信息www.ielts.org
测试内容的安排有两个主要目的
- o 学术 – 教育/专业目的
- o 培训 – 移民/培训目的

注册

- 注册可以在线上或者线下完成，全球超过140个国家有超过110个雅思考试中心，不同地区的注册费用也不同。考试当天必须向考试中心提交照片和有效证件。除了考试文件，笔，铅笔，橡皮和铅笔刀，其他任何纸质或者材料都不允许带入考场。

考试内容

- 雅思考试包含4部分。考试时间为两小时55分钟。
  - 听力部分需要在25-30分钟内（另外有10分钟誊写答案的时间）完成4个部分，40个问题。4部分内容分别是，
    - 第一部分为两个人的情景对话
    - 第二部分为一篇与社会话题相关的独白
    - 第三部分为四个人或少于四个人的教学/训练场景
    - 第四部分为一个教学/训练内容的独白
    - 不同的题目类型包括选择题，配对题，计划/地图/图表标签题，表格/笔记/图标/流程图/总结填空题，句子填空题以及简短问答题。
  - 阅读需要在60分钟内完成3个部分，4个问题。问题类型既有学术类的也有普通培训类的。
    - 学术类阅读的文章，会从书籍，专刊，杂志，报纸中摘取3段非专业的，具有普通标题的文章。
    - 普通培训类的三部分阅读材料，包含5-6个从通知，广告，工作简介，合同和员工发展，培训材料，时间表，报纸，杂志以及科幻或非科幻小说中摘取的内容。
    - 问题内容包括选择题，信息搜寻题，作者观点/要求搜寻题，信息/标题/特点/句末对应题，句子/摘要/笔记/图

表/流程图/图表标签填空和简短问答题。

- 写作部分需要在6分钟内完成2项任务。
    - 任务1是根据要求写一篇150词的短文，学术类考生需要描述所看到的信息（图表/表格/分析图/图解），而普通培训类考生需要根据已知情景写一封信。
    - 任务2是写一篇自由发挥的250词的短文，并对已知内容进行描述或提供相应观点。
- 口语部分包含3个部分，共11-14分钟。在这三个部分中，考生需回答每部分中的两个问题，这三部分的前半部的问题都类似，后一部分需要先做1分钟的准备，然后根据所给出的主题内容进行1-2分钟的演讲。
- 听力，阅读和写作是在同一天进行测试的。口语测试可以选择在测试前后7天内完成。

成绩 & 结果

- 具有两年有效期的成绩单会在测试后13天提供给考生，成绩单上会显示总成绩（1-9分），分项成绩（1-9分），考试类型以及个人信息。同时，也可以在线上查询成绩。

考试策略

这本书是通过有效的考试策略来帮助你提升成绩的指导教材。这本书有别于其他教材，例如学习指导或者练习测验。尽管我们提供了很多学习和练习测试问题的信息，但是这本书主要是讲解如果应对选择题。请不要担心 – 这并不是全部的内容！当你学习回答选择题的不同策略技巧时，你也可以练习你的阅读和听力理解能力，以及复习写作的技巧，要知道写作在整个雅思考试中占了超过一半的分值。

什么样的人能答好选择题？

面对选择题的多种挑战，你应当怎样做呢？有没有一种办法能提高正确率和分数呢？当然有！你读过这本书不会让你灰心丧气，而是让你注意到一些可以用于提升成绩的方法和策略。在详细讲解这些策略之前，我们先来看一看哪些人在这类考试中通常会有好的发挥。

了解考试材料的人。相信不用说大家也会知道，提高考试成绩最直接的方法就是熟知考试中会涵盖的材料内容。后面讲解的策略能够帮你解除心中的疑问，你需要做的是清楚了解你即将参加的考试要求，时间，名称和概念。

考试中冷静作答的人。紧张会导致你忘记一些你知道的信息。自信心对于选择题的发挥有极大的帮助。

考试前能够进行自我调节或祷告的人。这并不是在开玩笑。事实上在考前进行自我调节或者祷告的人，在进入考场之后会更有自信，在考试中也发挥的更出色一些。

在答题中运用逻辑而不是直觉的人。那些在考试中利用直觉答题的人，会容易因为感情用事而忽略掉事实。

能够系统作答的人。大多数指导教材都会涉及到这个问题，但是你不应该对于你不知道的问题进行胡乱猜测。你应该有一套系统的答题策略。

选择题快速答题技巧

在看具体方法之前，让我们来看一下有哪些你可以在考试以及不同类型选择题中使用的技巧。后面我们会进行具体的学习和研究。

不作弊也能找窍门 嘘。即使在考试中，你也可以找到解题的窍门 —— 并且是完全合法的。关键：利用测试本身的内容来找到答题的线索。你需要做的是，如果你不能找到问题的答案，可以尝试阅读答案的内容。如果从中你找到一个包含老师或者课本教授的知识点，有很大可能这就是正确的答案。原因是由于主题的复杂性，老师和课本通产会使用相同或类似的内容。

另一关键点：注意那些和前面问题相似的问题。通常来说，你会找到可以适用于多个问题的同一信息点。

有些时候，你会在一个问题中找到另一个问题的答案 – 因此要注意这类题型并使其成为你答题的优势。

在排除错误答案之前，试着先解决问题。如果你确定你的答案是正确的，那么就没有必要再去对错误答案进行筛选。如果你做不到这一点，那么看看你可以排除多少个选项。反复这个过程，看看能否接近正确选项。你选中正确答案的几率现在会大幅度提升。排除法是一个非常强大的方法，后面我们会进行深入的讨论和练习。

如果毫无头绪就先跳过。如果你不知道正确答案并且也不知道如何进行筛选，可以先在题目旁边做一个记号，等一下有时间的时候再返回来做。

排除那些概括性的，不能给出具体信息的答案。如果一个答案说，例如："Columbus came to the West in the spring"，一般来说就不是正确答案。

学会如何利用"all of the above" **和** "none of the above"。**如果是** "all of the above"，那么你需要检查所有选项来确保每一个都是正确的。先检查其中的两个。如果两个都是正确的，那么很大程度上所有答案都是正确的，因此你可以选择 "all"（当然，也会有例外的情况，特别是选项为 "A and B" 或者 "C and D"）。同样的，对于 "all of the above" 这类问题，你只要找出一个错误的选项，就可以删除两个选项 – 一个是错误的选项，另一个是 All of the Above 选项。

利用"接近的"答案来引导你。聪明的应试者之所以能够成功，是因为通常把两个接近的答案放在一起比较。聪明的应试者会利用这个方法来帮助他们找到正确的答案。如果你看到两个十分接近的答案，多数情况下它们之中的一个是正确的。也就是说你可以排除其他的选项 – 以此来提高你的正确率。例如，如果两个选项分别是 George Washington 和 George Washington Carver, Abraham Lincoln 以及 Thomas Edison，那么有极大可能两个含有Washington的答案中有一个是正确的。以下是关于这个方法的更多介绍。

当心陷阱问题

通常来说，大多数的问题都是通过表面进行选择，不应对其进行过度的分析。然而，大多数选择题测试，根据某些原因，都会包含一到两个陷阱题目。陷阱问题就是那些出题人故意让你觉得答案比实际答案要简单的题目。出题人出陷阱题目的原因，是因为大多数人认为他们已经掌握了考试技巧，没有必要再去学习其他的材料。只有很少的情况下考试中会出现很多的陷阱题目。那些被出题人加入到考试中的陷阱题目，只有在你对知识熟练彻底的掌握后才能正确作答。这也是区分"A"和"B+"学生，以及"A"与"A+"学生的区别。

解决陷阱问题最好的办法就是认真阅读题目并且把题目内容进行分割。然后再把分割后的部分分成单独的词。例如，如果问题说，"When a plane crashes on the border between the United States and Canada, where are the survivors buried?" 如果你逐一的观察每一个单词，你就会发现最后一个单词 "survivors" 指的是作者所说的生还者。

在你修改答案之前...

你现在可能熟悉了这个概念：你的第一直觉通常是对的。这也是为什么很多人，在给你考试建议的时候，告诉你说除非有足够的证据证明你的第一直觉是错误的，否则不要修改你的答案。一般在此类情况中，多数人会把本来正确的选项改成错误的，仅有一少部分能把错误的改成正确的。

如何处理这个问题。

让我们进一步来分析这个问题。也许你不是总想留下你第一个选择的答案，特别是当你有一个合理的机会证明你的第二选择是正确的时候。但是在修改你的答案之前，继续做后面的题目来整理一下你的思路。做过几道题目之后再回来重新看这个题目。看是不是你的原始答案仍然先闪出你的脑海。如果是的话，不要做任何修改。但如果这一次是第二个答案先在你的头脑中闪现，那么就改为第二个答案。如果觉得两个选项都正确，保持你的原始答案。

什么样的人能答好选择题？

面对选择题的多种挑战，你应当怎样做呢？有没有一种办法能提高正确率和分数呢？当然有！你读过这本书不会让你灰心丧气，而是让你注意到一些可以用于提升成绩的方法和策略。在详细讲解这些策略之前，我们先来看一看哪些人在这类考试中通常会有好的发挥。

> 了解考试材料的人。相信不用说大家也会知道，提高考试成绩最直接的方法就是熟知考试中会涵盖的材料内容。后面讲解的策略能够帮你解除心中的疑问，你需要做的是清楚了解你即将参加的考试要求，时间，名称和概念。
>
> 考试中冷静作答的人。紧张会导致你忘记一些你知道的信息。自信心对于选择题的发挥有极大的帮助。
>
> 考试前能够进行自我调节或祷告的人。这并不是在开玩笑。事实上在考前进行自我调节或者祷告的人，在进入考场之后会更有自信，在考试中也发挥的更出色一些。
>
> 在答题中运用逻辑而不是直觉的人。那些在考试中利用直觉答题的人，会容易因为感情用事而忽略掉事实。
>
> 能够系统作答的人。大多数指导教材都会涉及到这个问题，但是你不应该对于你不知道的问题进行胡乱猜测。你应该有一套系统的答题策略。

回答选择题的具体步骤

例题：

Which of the following is a helpful tip for taking a multiple-choice test?

    a. Answering "B" for all questions.

    b. Eliminate all answers that you know cannot be true.

    c. Eliminate all answers that seem like they might be true.

    d. Cheat off your neighbor.

如果你选择B，你的答案是正确的。即使你对答案不十分的确定，也要尽可能多的删除不正确的选项。以这种方式来思考：如果试卷中有四个有可能的选项，如果你从中猜选一个答案，你就有四分之一（25%）的概率选择到正确答案。也就是说你每猜四次就能够选择出正确答案。

然而，如果你能排除掉其中两个选项，你的几率就增大到二分之一，或者说50%。也就是说你每猜两次就能得到正确的答案。

对你的选择题成绩的提高，这个技巧的作用的是极大的。当然还有其他很多种你了解或不了解的技巧，同样会帮你提升成绩。但是要记住，这些技巧的使用都不是万无一失的。事实上，有一些了解这类技巧的出题人会故意出一些刁钻的题目来干扰你。然而通常来说，如果你能把这些技巧运用到联系中，那么你在考试中就会发挥的更好。

通过对这些技巧的熟练掌握，你可以提高你的正确率；或许能帮助你在成绩上提高积分来改变命运！

答题步骤

也许看起来有些复杂，或者觉得没有必要去依照公式来回答选择题。但是通过一段长时间的练习之后，你就会自然而然的使用它们，根本不会觉得麻烦。试着按照这些步骤来回答以下问题。

步骤1. 阅读题目的时候遮住答案。

在看选项之前在头脑中梳理一遍内容，并试着自己想象一下正确答案。

步骤2. 阅读答案。

步骤3. 排除或判断。
把你认为没有道理，不合逻辑或者有明显错误的选项划掉。之后再在剩下的选项中找正确答案。

步骤4. 注意干扰项。

干扰项是指和正确答案十分类似的选项，但是是用来迷惑你的。如果你看到两个选项特别相似，那么很大概率上正确选项就在他们之中。例如，如果问你正方形外侧距离的定义，给出的两个选项是"periwinkle"和"perimeter"，你可以猜测其中一个是正确答案，因为他们看起来很相似 （都是以"peri-"开始）。这样你猜中正确答案"perimeter"的概率就是50/50。

步骤5. 检查！

如果看到了你在脑中猜想过的答案，你可以在旁边做一个记号并看一看是否有其他更恰当的选项。如果没有，就可以选择你之前标记的选项。

步骤6. 如果毫无头绪，猜测一下。

如果你在脑中无法分析出正确答案，或者在尝试通过阅读文章来寻找答案后，你仍然对正确答案毫无头绪，那么可以试着猜一下。雅思考试中如果选错答案是不扣分的，所以猜也是一个好的策略之一。

很多人都听说选项"C"有更大的概率成为正确选项。如果是你的教授出题,这个逻辑也许能够成立,但是,现如今大多数标准化考试都是由电脑生成而且答案是随机分布的。所以选"C"这个策略我们并不建议使用。

以上就是选择题的快速热身介绍。下面,我们来看一下具体策略和练习题目。每一种策略都会被细致讲解,并附有相对应的练习题目。

答题卡

	A B C D E		A B C D E
1	○○○○○	26	○○○○○
2	○○○○○	27	○○○○○
3	○○○○○	28	○○○○○
4	○○○○○	29	○○○○○
5	○○○○○	30	○○○○○
6	○○○○○	31	○○○○○
7	○○○○○	32	○○○○○
8	○○○○○	33	○○○○○
9	○○○○○	34	○○○○○
10	○○○○○	35	○○○○○
11	○○○○○	36	○○○○○
12	○○○○○	37	○○○○○
13	○○○○○	38	○○○○○
14	○○○○○	39	○○○○○
15	○○○○○	40	○○○○○
16	○○○○○	41	○○○○○
17	○○○○○	42	○○○○○
18	○○○○○	43	○○○○○
19	○○○○○	44	○○○○○
20	○○○○○	45	○○○○○
21	○○○○○		
22	○○○○○		
23	○○○○○		
24	○○○○○		
25	○○○○○		

选择题答题策略练习题

以下是答题策略的具体讲解，每种策略后都附有练习题目。

每部分后面的答案都包括对每个策略和问题细致的讲解和讨论，以及回答技巧和内容分析。

策略1 – 定位关键词

对于每个问题来说，找到问题中的关键词对于理解问题的真正内容是至关重要的。划出关键词可以帮助你理清思路并记录相应内容的位置。

方法：阅读下面的文章，并用这个答题策略来回答问题。

Free-range is a method of farming where domesticated animals roam freely, or relatively freely, rather than being kept in a pen or cage. Free-range can mean two different things depending on who you talk to. One definition, when talking to a farmer, is a technical description of a farming method. You may have seen free-range or free-run eggs in the supermarket. This is a consumer oriented definition. There are numerous benefits to farmers who practice free-range farming. Certification as a free-range producer allows farmers to charge higher prices and also reduce feed costs. That's not all - free-range methods also improve the general health of animals, which produces a higher-quality product. In addition, free-range farming allows multiple crops on the same land - another significant savings for farmers. Free-range certification is different from organic certification.

1. **The free-range method of farming**

    a. Uses a minimum amount of fencing to give animals more room.

    b. Can refer to two different things.

    c. Is always a very humane method.

    d. Only allows for one crop at a time.

2. **Free-range farming is practiced**

    a. To obtain free-range certification.

    b. To lower the cost of feeding animals.

    c. To produce higher quality product.

    d. All of the above.

3. **Free-range farming:**

    a. Can mean either farmer described or consumer described methods.

    b. Is becoming much more popular in many areas.

    c. Has many limits and causes prices to go down.

    d. Is only done to make the animals happier and healthier.

4. **Free-range certification is most important to farmers because:**

    a. Free-range livestock are less expensive to feed.

    b. The price of the product is higher.

    c. Both a and b

    d. The animals are kept in smaller enclosures, so more can be produced.

策略2 – 注意否定词

对于每个问题来说，不论是哪种类型，一定要注意题目中的否定词。否定词包括 never, not, 以及任何其他会改变题目本身意思的词。

方法：阅读下面的文章，并用这个答题策略来回答问题。

Grizzly bears exhibit a common feature in nature, sexual dimorphism. This is where there are distinct difference in size or appearance between the sexes of an animal. Male grizzly bears, for example, generally weigh between 400 and 750 pounds, but can weight over 1,000 pounds. Females grizzlies are smaller, weighing 250 – 350 pounds, which is about 38% smaller. Female grizzlies stand about 3 feet at the shoulder, on all fours, and over 6 feet when standing upright. Males are bigger, generally standing 8 feet or more on their hind legs. Grizzlies in different geographical areas also show significant differences. For example, grizzlies from the Yukon River area in Northern Canada are 20% smaller.

5. Sexual dimorphism does not mean

    a. Male grizzly bears are the same size as the female of the species.

    b. All grizzly bears look the same and are the same size.

    c. Grizzly bears can be quite large, and weigh more than half a ton.

    d. All of the above

6. The size of a full-grown grizzly bear is never

    a. More than 500 pounds.

    b. Depends on the bear's sex.

    c. Determined simply by diet.

    d. Less than 8 feet tall.

7. Grizzly bears from the area of the Yukon River do not

    a. Get as big as most other grizzly bears do

    b. Get the rich and varied food supply needed

    c. Need the same nutrients as other grizzly bears

    d. Get less than 7 feet tall, and weigh close to half of a ton

策略3 – 认真阅读题干

对于每个问题来说，不论是哪种类型，阅读题干中的信息，然后在看选项之前试着自己先回答一下正确答案。

方法：阅读下面的文章，并用这个答题策略来回答问题。

Brown bears and grizzly bears are generally considered separate species, although technically, both are classified as Ursus Arctos. Brown bears live in coastal areas of North America where salmon is the primary food source. Bears found inland and in northern habitats are called 'grizzlies.' A sub species of Brown bears found on Kodiak Island, Alaska, have different shaped skulls due to the remote region and independent development.

Black bear, which are smaller and more common, are also a sub species, Ursus Americanus. Black bears are found throughout North America.

8. Grizzly bears, brown bears, and Kodiak bears are all

    a. Arctas Ursinas

    b. Ursus Arctos

    c. Arctos Ursina

    d. Ursula Arctic

9. Kodiak brown bears are classified as a different subspecies because

    a. They are much larger than other brown bears

    b. Their diet is radically different from that of other brown bears

    c. They are not true brown bears but instead a mixture of bear species

    d. Of their genetics and head shape, as well as their physical isolation

10. The term grizzlies, when referring to the brown bear, is used mainly

    a. In eastern areas where the bear grows large

    b. Only in snowy areas where there are low year round temperatures

    c. In the northern and inland areas

    d. In areas where the bear has a silver appearance

11. The term brown bear is normally used

a. When one of the main food sources is salmon

b. When the bear is small

c. When the bear is found inland

d. When the bear has a light brown coat and is very large

策略4 – 在做决定之前应考虑所有的选项

对于每个问题来说，不论是哪种类型，在下结论之前，确保你阅读了每一个选项。

方法：阅读下面的文章，并用这个答题策略来回答问题。

Polar bears and grizzlies are different species although there are rare cases of hybrids. Scientists have known the two species are compatible for some time and there are several cases of hybrids in zoos.

In 2006, in Canada's Northwest Territories, a hunter shot what he thought was a polar bear. This bear, however, was slightly different. Like most polar bears, its fur was thick and white, as one would expect of a polar bear. However the bear also had some characteristics of grizzlies, such as long claws, a humped back, and brown patches around its nose, eyes and back.

This odd combination of features from both species soon attracted attention of the Wildlife Genetics International in British Columbia, Canada, which confirmed that this animal was a polar bear grizzly hybrid through DNA testing, and, the first hybrid found in the wild.

This bear appears to be the product of a polar bear mother and a grizzly bear father. Until 2006, there had been no documented cases of a grizzly polar bear hybrid found in the wild.

12. Which grizzly bear features did the hybrid bear have?

    a. Brown patches in certain areas

    b. Long claws

    c. A shallow face

    d. All of the above

13. The hybrid bear was the result of

    a. A male brown bear and a female grizzly.

    b. A female brown bear and a male grizzly bear.

    c. A female polar bear and a male grizzly bear.

    d. A male polar bear and a female grizzly.

14. The hybrid bear tested here was

    a. The first case ever known where two different bear species mated successfully.

    b. Genetically flawed and prone to many diseases and conditions.

    c. A fluke, and a mistake of nature which has never happened.

    d. The first proof of a wild bear hybrid species outside zoos.

15. Modern science

a. Has proven that the cubs from two different species will not survive in almost every case.

b. Has known for some time that these hybrid bears were possible.

c. Completely understands how bear hybrids occur and why this happens in nature.

d. Has studied hundreds of bear hybrids in an attempt to learn more.

策略5 – 消除法

对于每个问题来说，不论是哪种类型，应先尽可能多的消除不正确的选项并缩窄选择范围。消除法应该是最有效的答题策略。

方法：阅读下面的文章，并用这个答题策略来回答问题。

Peacocks have been admired throughout history for their beautiful plumage and train of the male peafowl, or peacock, with its characteristic eye pattern.

In Greek mythology, Hera, wife of Zuess, and queen of the Gods, placed the hundred eyes of the slain giant Argus on the tail of the peacock, her favorite bird.

The peacock's tail or train, is not actually the tail, but the elongated feathers of the upper tail. These beautiful green-bronze feathers, with the eye pattern, can be seen when the train is fanned out. The actual tail feathers of the peacock are short and grey-colored and can be seen from behind when the train is fanned in a courtship display.

The grey tail feathers can also be seen during molting season, when males drop the feathers in their train. The female peacock is duller compared to the spectacular male. The female is brown, with some green iridescence feathers on her neck.

16. The long colorful tail feathers of the peacock

a. Are only present in the male of the species

b. Are used by both sexes to warn off predators

c. Are normally red and blue in color

d. Are only present for a very short time each year

17. The differences between the male and female peacock are

a. Size and weight

b. Coloring and tail feather length

c. The female does not ever leave the nest

d. The male sits on and hatches the eggs

18. The term peacock actually refers to

a. Both sexes from the pheasant family

b. The eyes on the tail feathers of the bird

c. The male bird of the peafowl species

d. The female bird of the peafowl species

19. The gray tail feathers on the male peacock can be seen

a. When the bird is startled

b. Only when the bird is searching for food

c. When the peacock lowers the tail feathers to the ground

d. During molting

策略6 – 对立法

对于每个问题来说，不论是哪种类型，认真阅读两个完全对立的选项。当两个选项出现相互对立的情况，他们其中的一个极有可能是正确选项。

方法：阅读下面的文章，并用这个答题策略来回答问题。

Smallpox is a highly infectious disease unique to humans, caused by two virus, Variola Major and Minor. The Latin name for smallpox is Variola or Variola Vera, which means spotted.

In 1980, the World Health Organization certified that Smallpox had been eradicated. Smallpox is sometimes confused with Chicken Pox, however, they are different virus.

The smallpox virus lives in the small blood vessels in the mouth, throat and skin. This gives a distinct rash in these areas, which turn into blisters. After being exposed to the Smallpox virus, symptoms do not appear for 12 to 17 days.

Variola Major is much more serious virus, with a mortality rate of 30 – 35%. Variola Minor is milder, with a mortality rate of only 1%. Variola Minor has several common names, including, alastrim, cotton-pox, milkpox, whitepox, and Cuban itch.

Variola Major causes several long-term complications such as scars, commonly on the face, which occurs in about 65 – 85% of the survivors. Other complications, including blindness and deformities from arthritis and other complications are much less common, about 2 – 5%.

20. Smallpox

    a. Effects all mammals, including humans

    b. Is caused by a bacteria from contact with dead flesh

    c. Was called the great pox during the fifteenth century

    d. Only affects humans, although other species can carry and transmit the virus

21. Smallpox caused by Variola major has a

    a. Thirty to thirty five percent survival rate

    b. Sixty percent mortality rate

    c. Thirty to thirty five percent mortality rate

    d. Sixty percent survival rate

22. Smallpox caused by Variola minor is

    a. Much more severe, with a greater number of pox and more scarring

    b. Much less severe, with fewer pox and less scarring

    c. Characterized because there are no pox

    d. So minor that no treatment or medical attention is needed

23. Smallpox can be fatal

a. In between thirty and thirty five percent of those who catch the virus, depending on the type

b. In between thirty and sixty five percent of those who catch the virus, depending on the type

c. When no medical treatment is available

d. Only in developing countries where medical care is poor

策略7 – 寻找不同

对于每个问题来说，不论是哪种类型，认真对比两个看起来十分接近的选项，然后认真分析它们之间的区别。对照题干来找出正确答案。

方法：阅读下面的文章，并用这个答题策略来回答问题。

Lightning is one of the most amazing natural phenomenon. A popular belief is that lightning cannot strike twice in the same place. This however, is not true - lightning does strike in the same place frequently.

Lightning is an electrical discharge between clouds and the ground, or between two clouds. It is often accompanied with thunder during thunderstorms, dust storms and volcanic eruptions. Every year, there are an estimated 16 million lightning storms worldwide.

Bolts of lightning travel at speeds of 130,000 miles per hour and contain a billion volts of electricity. Lightning bolts can reach temperatures of 54,000° F. This is hot enough to turn sand, some soils or even rock into hollow glass channels, called fulgurites. Fulgurites extend far below the surface.

Lightning is such a common feature of the natural world, there is even a classification for the fear of lightning and thunder, called astraphobia.

Clouds of volcanic ash, as well as dust storms and forest fires can generate enough static electricity to produce lightning.

Scientists do not understand the process of lightning formation, and this is a matter for debate. Scientists have studied causes of lightning, such as wind, humidity, friction, atmospheric pressure, solar winds and accumulation of charged solar particles. Many scientists believe that ice inside clouds is important in causing lightning.

24. Astraphobia is

    a. Fear of thunder

    b. Fear of thunder and lightning

    c. Fear of lightning

    d. None of the above

25. Lightning occurs

    a. Only in thunderstorms

    b. In thunderstorms and dust storms

    c. In thunderstorms, volcanic eruptions and dust storms

    d. In the upper atmosphere

26. Fulgurites are

a. Made of silica

b. Made of glass

c. Made of silica turned in to glass

d. Made of silica and glass

策略8 – 文章线索

结合句子和文章内容来找出最佳答案。有些时候，题目的答案可能就在文章或问题当中。

方法：阅读下面的文章，并用这个答题策略来回答问题。

Venus is one of the four solar terrestrial planets, or rocky bodies that orbit the sun. Planets are defined as a celestial body moving in an elliptical orbit around a star. Venus is about the same size as Earth. Venus' diameter (12,104 km) is only 650 km. less than Earth's, (12,742 km.) and its mass is 81.5% of Earth's. The Venusian atmosphere is a dense mixture of carbon dioxide with some nitrogen.

Venus orbits the sun every 224.7 days, and is the second-closest planet to the Sun.

Venus, as the second brightest star in the sky, reaching an apparent magnitude of −4.6, was named after Venus, the goddess of love and beauty by the Romans. The Romans named all the brightest stars after their Gods and Goddesses. Venus is often called the Morning, or Evening Star. Venus reaches its maximum brightness before sunrise and after sunset

Venus is an inferior planet from Earth, meaning that

it is closer to the sun: its elongation reaches a maximum of 47.8°.

27. Apparent magnitude is

    a. A measure of darkness

    b. A measure of brightness

    c. The distance from the moon

    d. The distance from the earth

28. The elongation of a planet is

    a. The angular distance from the sun, as seen from earth.

    b. The distance from the sun

    c. The distance form the earth

    d. None of the above

29. Terrestrial planets are

    a. Made of rock b. Have people on them

    c. The earth and no others

    d. The same size as Earth

30. How many planets orbit the sun in less than 224.7 days?

    a. 1 planet

    b. Only Venus

    c. 2 planets

    d. 3 planets

策略 9 – 测试每一个选项

对于定义类题目，要测试所有的选项 – 其中一个会比其他的选项都合适。当你阅读选项的时候，可以使用策略5 – 排除法来排除明显错误的选项。

方法：阅读下面的文章，并用这个答题策略来回答问题。

Some of the common weather patterns on Earth are rain, wind, fog, and snow. Other weather patterns, generally classified as natural disasters, are hurricanes, tornadoes, typhoons and ice storms. Weather generally happens in the lower portion of the atmosphere, called the troposphere. Some weather can occur in the upper atmosphere, or stratosphere, where it can effect weather in the lower troposphere.

The principle cause of weather is different temperature, barometric pressure and moisture densities in the atmosphere. Weather phenomena in the atmosphere such as the jet stream is caused by the temperature differences in the tropical and polar air, which causes air to move from one to the other. The jet stream generally flows in a Western direction, and there are two or three jet streams in the Northern and Southern Hemispheres at any time.

Instabilities in the flow of the jet stream cause weather systems such as extra-tropical cyclones. Different processes cause weather systems such as monsoons or thunderstorms. Monsoons are caused by a difference in temperature over land and over sea.

Due to the tilt of the Earth's axis, sunlight reaches the Earth at different angles at different times of the year, creating seasons. In January, the Northern Hemisphere is tilted away from the sun, so sunlight is more direct than in July.

31. The troposphere is

a. The highest strata of the atmosphere
b. The lowest strata of the atmosphere
c. The middle level of the atmosphere
d. Not part of the atmosphere

32. Monsoons are

a. Caused by instabilities in the jet stream
b. Caused by processes other than instabilities in the jet stream
c. Part of the jet stream
d. Cause the jet stream

33. Extra-tropical cyclones occur

a. In the tropics
b. In temperate zones
c. In the gulf stream
d. In mid-latitudes

34. Tilted means:

a. Slanted
b. Rotating
c. Connected to
d. Bent

策略10 – 寻找细节

对于需要细节支持的题目，寻找细节是解题的关键。阅读文章并锁定正确选项。永远不要忘记你看到的选项是用来迷惑你的，甚至有的看起来是合情合理的。然而，如果文章中没有提到过，它们就属于"干扰"选项。

最佳答案是在文章中可以找到相应内容的答案。

方法：阅读下面的文章，并用这个答题策略来回答问题。

Ebola is a common term for a group of viruses in the genus Ebola (EBOV), family Filoviridae. There are several species within the Ebola virus genus, with specific strains. Ebola is also a general term for the disease the viruses cause, Ebola hemorrhagic fever. The Ebola virus is transmitted through bodily fluids.

The Ebola viruses are similar to the Marburg virus, also in the family Filoviridae. Most viruses are spherical, however, the Ebola viruses have long filaments. The Ebola and Marburg viruses have similar symptoms.

The first outbreak of Ebola occurred near the Ebola River, in the Democratic Republic of the Congo, which the disease and viruses are named after. Ebola is a very serious illness, very contagious and often fatal. The 2014 West African Ebola viral epidemic was the most widespread in history.

The Zaire virus was the first discovered in 1976 and is the most lethal. Ebola first emerged in 1976 in Zaire. An outbreak in Reston, Virginia brought the virus to international attention.

35. The Ebola virus received this name because of

    a. The doctor who first discovered the virus

    b. The cure that is used to treat those infected

    c. The river where the disease was first encountered

    d. What the virus does to the body

36. Viruses in the Ebola genus are recognizable

    a. Because of their hooked shape

    b. Because of their long filaments

    c. Due to their oblong heads

    d. Because of their unique color

37. One of the most common causes of death from the Ebola family of viruses is

    a. Hypovolemic shock due to blood vessel damage

    b. Bleeding of the brain that cannot be stopped

    c. A heart attack from blood loss and lack of fluids

    d. A high fever that cannot be lowered

38. The most deadly strain of the Ebola virus family is the

    a. The Reston strain

    b. The Ivory Coast strain

    c. The Zaire strain

    d. The Sudan strain

策略11 – 宏观策略

在回答中心思想和总结性问题的时候,细节可能会对你造成迷惑,但是不要让这些细节使你分心。避开细节部分,使用统揽全文的宏观策略找出正确答案。

方法:阅读下面的文章,并用这个答题策略来回答问题。

In 2005 researchers found three species of fruit bat carrying the Ebola virus, but not showing disease symptoms. These three species are called natural host, or reservoir species. Scientists have studied plants, insects and birds as potential reservoir species without success. Bats are the only reservoir species scientists have found. . Apparently, bats are reservoir species for several viruses.

The first outbreaks, in 1976 and 1979, were in cotton factories where bats lived. Bats were also present in the Marburg infections in 1975 and 1980.

39. The species most suspected as a potential Ebola virus reservoir is

    a. Birds
    b. Insects
    c. Plants
    d. Bats

40. Most plant and animal species

a. Can carry the Ebola virus but not become infected

b. Can not carry and transmit the Ebola virus

c. Are responsible for new cases of Ebola viruses

d. Can be infected with one of the Ebola viruses

41. Bats are known for

a. Being carriers of many different viruses, including Ebola

b. Transmitting the Ebola virus through a scratch

c. Being susceptible to the virus and becoming infected

d. Transmitting the Ebola virus through infected droppings

策略12 – 最佳答案

尝试根据文章的信息内容找到最佳答案。不要被看似正确或看似比较正确的选项所干扰。

方法：阅读下面的文章，并用这个答题策略来回答问题。

In the early stages, Ebola may not be highly contagious. Contact with someone in early stages may not even transmit the disease. As the illness progresses, bodily fluids represent an extreme biohazard.

Due to lack of proper equipment and hygienic practices, large-scale epidemics occur mostly in poor, isolated areas without modern hospitals or well-educated medical staff. Many areas where the infectious reservoir exists have just these characteristics.

In such environments, all that can be done is immediately cease all needle sharing or use without adequate sterilization procedures, to isolate patients, and to observe strict barrier nursing procedures with the use of a medical-rated disposable face mask, gloves, goggles, and a gown always. This should be strictly enforced for all medical personnel and visitors.

42. Ebola is highly contagious

a. Only when blood is present

b. Only in the first stages before hemorrhaging occurs

c. At all stages of the illness from incubation to recovery

d. Only in the later stages when the virus is very numerous

43. Exposure to the Ebola virus means

a. A death sentence for most patients

b. Isolation for the patient, and proper precautions for all medical personnel to contain the virus

c. The virus will spread rapidly and there is no treatment available

d. A full recovery usually, with very few symptoms

44. Ebola outbreaks commonly occur

a. Because sterilization and containment procedures are not followed or available

b. Due to infected animals in the area

c. Because of rat droppings in homes

d. Because of a contaminated water supply

45. Ebola is

a. More common in advanced nations where treatment makes the disease minor

b. More common in third world and developing countries

c. Fatal in more than ninety-five percent of the cases

d. Highly contagious during the incubation period

应答键

策略1 – 定位关键词

1. B
题目问到 the free range method of farming。这里的 method 指的是 type of farming。"Method" 是这个题目的关键词，应该对它做出相应标记。

The question asks about the free range *method* of farming. Here method refers to *type* of farming. "Method" here is the keyword and can be marked or underlined.

2. D
这道题目 "Free-range farming is practiced..."，这里的关键词是 "practiced"。在答案中我们发现所有的选项都是以 "to" 开头的，所以不难发现题目是在问 why free range ...，其中有一个选项是 "All of the above" 就是这道题的正确答案。然而，当 "All of the above" 出现在选项中时，我们可以采用排除法。你需要做的是，只要找到一个不正确的选项，就可以使用策略5 – 排除法来排除其中的两个选项，把你的选择范围从四选一变成二选一。

The Question is, "Free-range farming is *practiced* ..." The keyword here is "practiced." Looking at the choices, which all start with "to," it is clear the answer will be about *why* free range ... Also notice that one choice is "All of the above," which here, is the correct answer. However, when "All of the above" is an option, this is a potential Elimination Strategy. Simply find one choice that is incorrect and you can use Strategy 5 - Elimination to eliminate two choices and increase your odds from one in four, to one in two.

3. A
这个题目是，"Free range farming husbandry…"问题中缺少关键词，所以根据选项中的内容，答案应该是自由放牧型农业的定义。

The question is, "Free range farming husbandry …" From the question, and the *lack* of keywords, together with the choices presented, the answer will be a definition free range farming husbandry.

4. C
这道题目是，"Free-range certification is most important to farmers because…"这里的关键词是"most important"。要注意，应从选项中挑选出最佳的答案。

The question is, "Free-range certification is *most important* to farmers because … " The keywords here are "most important." Circle the keywords to keep them clear in your mind. Be careful to choose the best possible answer.

策略2 – 注意否定词

这四个问题中都包含否定的提问：does not mean, is never, do not, and is not。这些问题可以用排除可能性的方法来解决，所以如果你看到任何正确的选项，可以立刻排除。

5. D
这个问题问的是sexual dimorphism does not mean。用笔圈出"not"并时刻提醒自己。然后，找出什么是sexual dimorphism。快速阅读文章，sexual dimorphism并没有给出直接的定义，而是举例说明母熊相对于公熊的体型较小。也许在不同的方面会有不同的定义，但是广义上的定义就是这道题目的答案。首先，注意"All of the above"是选项D。除此之外，这道题属于否定类题目。所以如果选项D正确，选项A,B或C必须都是错误的，这样你才能排除其他三项而选择D。
经过验证，三项都是不正确的，所以选项D "All of the above" 是正确答案。

选项A，雌性和雄性体型相等是不正确的。

The question asks what sexual dimorphism does *not* mean. Circle the word "not" and keep it firmly in mind. Next, what is sexual dimorphism. Reading the text quickly, sexual dimorphism is related to the female bears being smaller than the males. Probably there are other aspects, but this general definition is all that is needed to answer the question.

First, notice that "All of the above" is choice D. In addition, the question is a negative. So, for choice D to be correct, choices A, B and C must be *in*correct. This narrows down your options. If any of choices A, B or C are correct, then you can eliminate that choice as well as choice D.

Either all the choices are *in*correct, in which case, choice D, "All of the above" is correct.

Choice A, male and females are the same size is incorrect.
Choice B, all grizzly bears look the same and are the same size, is incorrect. Choice C, grizzly bears (plural so *all* grizzly bears) can be large and weigh more than half a ton. This is incorrect since while all grizzly bears are large, female bears weight less than half a ton.

All three choices are incorrect so choice D is the correct answer, "All of the Above," are incorrect.

6. A

首先，圈出或者划出never来提示自己这是一道关于否定的题目。然后从选项中找到不正确的一项。

选项A 是正确的，因为 male bears are 1,000 pounds。在这个选项旁边做一个标记。也许你在此刻非常想选择这个选项，但是在做出最终决定前看清每一个选项的内容是十分重要的。

选项B 是不正确的 - size does not depend on the sex.
选项C 是不正确的 - size does not depend on diet.
选项D 是不正确的 - males often stand 8 feet.
因此选项A是正确选项。

First, circle or underline never to show this is a negative question. Now look at the options to find an option that is not true.

Choice A is true as male bears are 1,000 pounds. Place a mark beside this one. It may be tempting to select this option as your answer, but it is important to look at all choices before making a final decision.

Choice B is not true - size does not depend on the sex.
Choice C is not true - size does not depend on diet.
Choice D is not true - males often stand 8 feet.

So choice A is correct.

7. A

首先圈出"do not"来提示自己这是一道关于否定的题目。
选项A是正确的，Yukon River grizzly bears do not get as big as other grizzlies, 所以先在选项旁边标上记号以供参考。选择答案之前要阅读其他选项的内容。
选项B在文章中找不到相应的出处，因此可以被排出掉。
选项C也在文章中找不到相应的出处，因此也可以被排出掉。

选项D的描述是正确的，但是这是一道否定类问题，所以这个选项是错误的。

以上的某些选项也许从常识的角度看是属于正确的，但是由于在文章中并无提及，因此可以被排出掉。

选项A是正确的答案。

First circle "do not" to mark this as a negative question.

Choice A is correct, Yukon River grizzly bears do not get as big as other grizzlies, so mark it for later consideration. Examine the other choices before making a final decision.

Choice B is not mentioned in the text, and can be eliminated.

Choice C is not mentioned in the text and can be eliminated.

Choice D is true, but this is a negative question so it is false.

Some of the above choices may be true from a common sense point of view, but if they aren't mentioned specifically in the passage, they can be eliminated.

Choice A is correct.

策略3 – 认真阅读题干。

首先阅读问题，然后在看选项之前，试着在文章中找到相应答案。先读选项会干扰你的思路，正如它们使用在选项中的作用一样！

8. B
这个选项是故意用来迷惑人的！拉丁物种中4种名称的变化，给出的是Ursus Arctos，题目问哪一个拉丁名称的版本是正确的，这里给出了一个非常直接的解题思路。因为名字是拉丁文，它们在文章中会十分的显眼。先看第一个选项，"Arctas Ursinas，" 然后快速浏览全文并试着找到和它相似的词。在第二句的结尾你会看到一个非常接近的词 "Ursus Arctos" 。之后找到这个词在句子中所指的词，所以B是正确答案。

The choices here are very confusing and are meant to be! Four variations on the latin species name, Ursus Arctos are given, so the question is what version of this latin name is correct, which gives a very straight-forward strategy to solving. Since the name is latin, it is going to stand out in the text. Take the first option, "Arctas Ursinas," and scan the text for something that looks like that. At the end of the second sentence is "Ursus Arctos," which is very close. Next confirm what this sentence refers to, which gives the correct answer, Choice B.

9. D
这个问题是为什么Kodiak brown bears属于不同的亚种，选项设计的目的是为了迷惑那些粗心和焦虑的考生。快速浏览文章，你会在第二句和最后一句之间找到"Kodiak"，通过这几句可以找到答案。

This question asks why Kodiak brown bears are a different subspecies, and the options are designed to confuse a careless, stressed test-taker. Scan the text for "Kodiak," which appears in the second to last sentence, and answers the question.

10. C
这个问题问的是brown bears和grizzly bears的区别。如果你不细心，就会落入选项中设计的陷阱。

This question asks about the relationship between brown bears and grizzly bears. If you are not careful you will be confused by the choices.

11. A
阅读题目后，为避免选项的干扰，先通过浏览文章来找出题目答案。

Read the question, then read the text before trying to answer and avoid confusion.

策略4 – 作答之前阅读所有的选项

在策略3中，我们学习到了在读选项之前，先试着自己在文章中找到正确答案。好，那么现在你阅读了文章并找到的正确答案。下一步就是策略4 – 阅读所有的选项。当阅读所有选项的内容后，选择出正确的答案。

12. D
首先，要注意"All of the above"是其中的一项。所以只要你找到一个不正确的选项，你就能排出选项D "All of the above"。首先是阅读题目，（策略3）接着是浏览文章，然后在作答前阅读所有的选项 Reading the question first, (Strategy #3) then looking in the text, and then reading all，你会发现选项A，B和C都是正确的，所以选项D，All of the Above，是正确的选项。

First, notice that "All of the above" is a choice. So if you find one option that is incorrect, you can eliminate that choice and choice D, "All of the above." Reading the question first, (Strategy #3) then looking in the text, and then reading all the choices before answering, you can see that choices A, B and C are all correct, so choice D, All of the Above, is the correct choice.

If you had not read all the choices first, then you might be tempted to impulsively choose A, B, or C.

13. C
设计出不同选项的目的是通过不同的选择和组合内容来迷惑你。认清这一点之后，因此在你找出选项的时候一定要非常的细心。如果你很紧张，很着急，或者不注重细节的话，你可能就会由于冲动或者没有通读全文而选择出错误的答案。在文章中，你会找到 "This bear appears to be the product of a polar bear mother and a grizzly bear father." 这个句子，这里给出了问题的答案。

Looking at the choices, they are designed to confuse with different choices and combinations. Recognizing this, it is therefore important to be extra careful in making your choice. If you are stressed, in a hurry, or not paying attention, you will probably get this question wrong by making an impulsive choice and not reading through all the choices before making a selection.

Referring to the text, you will find the sentence, "This bear appears to be the product of a polar bear mother and a grizzly bear father." which answers the question.

14. D
阅读所有的选项，B和C可以被立刻排除掉，因为他们没有在文章中的依据。由于在文章中找不到相关的内容，所以即使他们看起来合理，也应被排除掉。

再来看选项A和D，他们之间的不同是 if this has happened before, or has it happened only in zoos。回到文章中，最后一句话给出了答案，Until 2006, there had been no documented cases of a grizzly polar bear hybrid found in the wild."

Reading through all the choices, B and C can be eliminated right away as they are not mentioned in the text. They might appear as good answers but they are not from the passage.

Looking at choices A and D, the issue is if this has happened before, or has it happened only in zoos. Referring to the text, the second paragraph tells us it is the first hybrid found in the wild.

15. B
阅读四个选项，问题问的是 what does science know? Does it happen all the time? Completely understood? They do survive? Is it possible? 试着在文章中找到与 how much is known相关的内容。从最后一句话中 "Until 2006, there had been no documented cases of a grizzly polar bear hybrid found in the wild."，我们可以找到答案。

Reading through the four choices, the question concerns, what does science know? Does it happen all the time? Completely understood? They do survive? Is it possible? Look in the text for how much is known. The last sentence, "Until 2006, there had been no documented cases of a grizzly polar bear hybrid found in the wild." gives the answer.

策略5 – 消除法

对于每个问题来说，不论是哪种类型，应先尽可能多的消除不正确的选项并缩窄选择范围。消除法应该是最有效的答题策略。

16. A
利用这个策略我们可以将选项A和D排出。我从来没有见过尾巴是红色的孔雀，所以选项C应该也可以被排除掉，但是先不要下定论。对于大多数的鸟类和动物来说，一般都是雄性的颜色较为鲜艳，而雌性的比较不鲜艳。选项B之所以是错误的是因为选项中说"both sexes" having colorful tails。选项D可以被考虑为正确选项是因为文章中对molting season做了描述，然而，文章中并没有提及时间的长短，因此这个选项存在一定的疑问。这样一来，选项A就成为了最佳的选择，因为在文章中有与其直接对应的内容。

Using this strategy the choices can be narrowed down to choices A and D. The text doesn't mention red in the tail, so choice C can be eliminated. Choice B can be eliminated as it refers to "both sexes" having colorful tails. Choice D is a good candidate as the text refers to molting season, however, the text does not say how long this is, so there is some doubt. This makes choice A the best choice as it is referred to directly in the text.

17. B
因为对于雄鸟一般不会卧在蛋上，所以选项D可以立刻被排除掉。

快速浏览文章，你会发现没有与选项A和C直接相关的内容，因此这两个选项可以被排除掉。

Choice D can be eliminated right away, as a male bird to sit on eggs is not mentioned in the text.

Skimming the passage, choices A and C can be eliminated, as they are not mentioned directly in the text, leaving only choice D.

18. C
Choices A, B and D can be eliminated right away, as the passage states the peacock is the male bird. Referring to the text, "plumage and train of the male peafowl, or peacock …" making choice C the best choice.

19. D
选项A和B可以立刻被排除掉，或者可以通过快速在文章中进行确认，你会发现文章中没有任何线索。选项C是可疑选项是因为the grey feathers are under the tail feathers …，因此当尾部的羽毛位置很低时，灰色的羽毛是很难被观察到的。

Choices A and B can be eliminated either right away or with a quick check of the passage, since they are not mentioned. Choice C is suspicious since the grey feathers are under the tail feathers, so it is difficult to see how they could be visible when the tail feathers are lowered.

策略6 – 对立选项

如果选项中有对立项，通常来说其中一个就是正确的答案。如果这样有帮助的话，可以做一个表格，将所有的对立选项都写进去，这样正确的选项就一目了然了。

20. D
这里要注意A和D是对立选项。回到文章中，"Smallpox is an infectious disease unique to humans …" 证明选项A是错误的。并且选项B和C在文章中完全没有提到过，因此也可以被排除掉。
Notice that choices A and D are opposites. Referring

to the text, "Smallpox is a highly infectious disease unique to humans ..." eliminates choice A. Also notice choices B and C are not mentioned in the text and can be eliminated right away.

21. C
这里面所有的选项都是对立的。30 - 35% mortality, or survival rate, or 60%。因此解题方法就是阅读文章，寻找30%或者60%，survival或者mortality，保持头脑清醒，不要迷惑。有的时候笔记和表格对于理清思路是很有帮助的。

题目问的是百分比，所以最简单快速的办法就是快速浏览文章并找到百分比的标志。

第一个百分比的标志位于第二段，30% - 35%。先在旁边做上记号。 然后，通过分析这个百分比在文中指的是mortality rate。所以在30 - 35%旁边写下mortality。现在，反向搜索文章内容，看一看30 - 35% mortality指的是什么。在句子的开头可以找到所指的是Variola Major。

| 30 – 35% | Mortality | V. Major |

通过快速简单的搜索，现在我们清楚的知道文章真正想表达的内容，并且希望我们不会被不同的选项所迷惑。
选项A和B可以被立刻排除。选项C看起来是正确的。快速检查选项D以确保这个选项是不正确的。因此选项C是正确答案。

Notice that all the choices are opposites. 30% - 35% mortality, or survival rate, or 60%. Therefore, the task is to review the text, looking for 30% or 60%, survival or mortality, stay clear, and do not get confused. Sometimes making notes or a table can help to clarify.
The question is asking about percent, so it is easy and fast to skim the passage for a percent sign.

The first percent sign is in the fourth paragraph, 30% - 35%. Write this in the margin. Next, see what this percent refers to, which is the mortality rate. Write "mortality" next to 30% - 35%. Now, working backwards, see what the 30% - 35% mortality rate refers to. At the beginning of that sentence, is Variola Major.

| 30% - 35% | Mortality | V. Major |

Now we have a clear understanding of what the passage is saying, which we have retrieved quickly and easily, and hopefully will not be confused by the different choices.

Choices A and B can be eliminated right away. Choice C looks correct. Check choice D quickly, and confirm that it is incorrect. Choice C is the correct answer.

22. B
选项A和B是对立选项。Is Variola Minor more or less severe, with more or fewer pox, and more or less scarring? 其他两个选项"no pox"和"no treatment"可以被立刻排除。选项A或B都的任何一个都有可能是错误的。
快速做一个图表：

Major - more serious - scars, blindness
Minor - milder

文章中没有提及Variola minor会造成scarring，但是我们可以推测milder才会。现在来看一下选项，选项A清楚的谈论到Variola major，所以我们推测选项B谈论的是Variola minor，也就是正确的答案。当然我们也可以通过文章内容来印证我们的推测。

这里还要注意 'major' 和 'minor' 这两个词，它们可以对事物的严重程度提供思路，因此选项A可以被排除。

Choices A and B are opposites. Is Variola Minor more or less severe, with more or fewer pox, and more or less scarring? The other two choices, "no pox" and "no treatment" can be eliminated quickly. Either choice A or B are going to be wrong.

Make a quick table like this:

Major - more serious - scars, blindness
Minor - milder

The passage does not mention scarring from Variola minor, but we can infer that it is milder. Looking at the options, choice A is clearly talking about Variola major, and we can infer that choice B is talking about Variola minor and is the correct answer. We can confirm our inference from the text.

Also note the words, 'major' and 'minor.' Which gives a clue concerning severity, and the elimination of choice A.

23. A

选项A和B并不是完全对立的选项，而是非常接近的，如果你不能正确理解它们的意思，你就会被它们所迷惑，这也是这个题目设计的目的。How many people die from the virus? Between 30 and 35%? Or between 35 and 60%? 记住这些数字然后快速浏览全文。这个问题问的是一个百分比，所以快速浏览文章寻找百分比的标志，你会在第二段的一开始有所发现。然后反向阅读句子，你会找到这个百分比在文中指的是mortality。

Choices A and B are not exactly opposite, but very

close and designed to confuse if you do not read them properly. How many people die from the virus? Between 30% and 35%? Or between 35% and 60%? Scan the text with these numbers in mind.

This question is asking about a percent, so quickly scan the passage for a percent sign, which first appears in the second paragraph. Working back, confirm that the percent figures that you quickly found is related to mortality, which it is.

策略7 – 寻找不同

当看到两个十分接近的答案时，认真寻找它们之间的不同。

24. B
选项A，B和C之间非常的接近，设计它们的目的就是为了迷惑和扰乱那些不仔细阅读文章的考生。What is astraphobia exactly? 这是一道关于生僻词astraphobia的定义类题目。在文章中搜索"astraphobia"，你会发现选项B是正确答案。

Choices A, B and C are very similar and designed to confuse and distract someone who does not look carefully at the text. What is astraphobia exactly? This is a definition question for an unusual word, astraphobia. Scan the text for "astraphobia." Choice B is correct.

25. C

选项A，B和C之间非常的接近，它们设计的目的是为了迷惑考生，或者用来诱惑压力大或不细心的考生，让他们快速的选出错误的选项。通篇浏览文章，在第一段中你会找到 lightning occurs in thunderstorms, volcanic eruptions and in dust storms，所以选项C是正确的。

Choices A, B and C are similar and designed to confuse, or tempt a stressed or careless test-taker into making a quick and incorrect choice. Checking the passage, in the first paragraph, lightning occurs in thunderstorms, volcanic eruptions and in dust storms, so choice C is correct.

26. C

所有的选项之间都是相似的并用来迷惑考生的。看看他们之间的相似程度是多少，因为区分不同定义之间的区别十分重要。快速浏览文章来寻找"fulgurites"这个词。在第一段你会找到 "This is hot enough to turn sand, some soils or even rock into hollow glass channels…" 所以能够正确回答问题的最佳选项是选项C "Made of silica turned into glass"。

26. C

All four answers are similar and designed to confuse. Seeing how similar the choices are, it is very important to be clear on the exact definition. Scan the text quickly for the word "fulgurites." From the third paragraph, "This is hot enough to turn sand, some soils or even rock into hollow glass channels…" so the correct answer, and the option that answers the question best, is choice C.

策略8 – 文章线索

结合句子和文章来判断出最佳的答案。有的时候，问题的答案可能就隐藏在文章或题目中。

27. B
你不需要精准了解文章的意思 – 只要能够回答问题就可以了。文章中有这样的描述 "Venus, as the second brightest star in the sky, reaching an apparent magnitude of -4.6, was named after Venus"，所以金星是用来和月球的亮度做比较的，因此视星等一定和行星的亮度有关系，这样我们就有足够的信息来回答问题了。还要注意的是选项彼此之间的相对性。选项A和B于选项C和D之间是相对的两组选项。

You do not have to know the exact meaning - just enough to answer the question. The phrase is used in the passage, "Venus, as the second brightest star in the sky, after the moon, reaches an apparent magnitude of −4.6 …" where Venus is compared to the brightness of the moon, so the apparent magnitude must have something to do with brightness, which is enough information to answer the question. Notice also, how the choices are opposites. Choice A and B are opposites as are choices C and D.

28. A
精准的意思不是必须要了解的，只要你能有足够的信息来回答问题就可以了。文章中的原始描述是这样的"Venus is an inferior planet from Earth, meaning that it is closer to the sun: its elongation reaches a maximum of 47.8°." 句子中的Elongation是天体离太阳的角距离，并且和地球也有一定的关系。选项C可以被立刻排除掉，因为已经有一个错误的选项，所以选项D，All of the Above也可以被排除掉。选项A是最正确的答案，因为在文章中提到了"as seen from earth"。

The exact meaning is not necessary, you only need only enough information to answer the question. The passage where this phrase is used is, "Venus is an inferior planet from Earth, meaning that it is closer to the sun: its elongation reaches a maximum of 47.8°." Elongation in this sentence is something connected with distance from the sun, but also something to do with Earth. Choice C can be eliminated right away, and since one choice is wrong, Choice D, All of the Above, can also be eliminated. Choice A is the best answer since it mentions, "as seen from earth."

29. A
选项C和D可以被同时排除掉。文章中没有任何关于尺寸和任务的信息，所以选项C和D都是不正确的。Terrestrial有很多类似的定义，但是选项A是最佳的选项。从文章中我们可以找到"Venus is one of the four solar terrestrial planets, or rocky bodies that orbit the sun."。

这里要注意选项B是有语法错误的，因此也可以被排除掉。题目的内容是"Terrestrial planets are," 而选项B的内容是 "Have people on them."。

通过判断语法错误来排出选项是一个非常好的策略，你有可能会希望看到这些由教授们出题时所犯的错误。然而，大多数标准化考试都是由电脑生成，之后会由大量专业的人员进行校对和修改，以避免类似的低级错误的发生。既然这些属于低级错误，所以在真正的标准化考试时是不会出现的。

Choices C and D can be eliminated right away. No mention is made of size or people, so choices C and D are also incorrect. Terrestrial has many similar meanings, but choice A is the best. From the passage, "Venus is one of the four solar terrestrial planets, or rocky bodies that orbit the sun."

Note that choice B is a grammatical error and can be eliminated right away. The question is, "Terrestrial planets are," and choice B is, "Have people on them."

This is a great strategy, looking for grammatical errors and eliminating, and what you might expect to see on a test that a professor has made themselves. However, most standardized tests are generated by computer, and proofed by many different people who have considerable expertise in correcting this type of easy question. Keep this in mind because it is an easy elimination, but don't expect to see this type of thing on a standardized test.

30. A
这是一道用来迷惑考生的陷阱题，因为回答这道题需要使用额外的逻辑步骤。根据文章的内容，Venus是离太阳第二近的行星，因此肯定有另外一个行星离太阳更近。离太阳更近的行星的绕太阳的环行速度会更快，所以选项A一定是正确选项。

This is a bit of a trick question and designed to confuse, as it requires an additional step of logical reasoning. Referring to the text, Venus is the *second* closest planet to the sun so there must be one planet that is closer. Planets closer to the sun will rotate the sun faster, so the answer must be choice A

策略9 – 词义理解题要参考所有选项

对于定义类的问题，一定要参考所有的选项 – 因为其中一个选项的解释可能比其他选项都恰当。当你阅读选项的时候，使用策略5 – 消除法，来消除你觉得明显不正确的选项。

31. B
答案可以从文章中直接获取。这里要注意选项A和B是对立的两个选项，所以它们其中有一个一定是不正确的。认真在文章中寻找准确的定义。如果你对答案不确定，可以在边缘处做一个表格。快速浏览文章来寻找需要定义的目标词汇。一些大的词和不常见的词可以很容易的被发现和定位。 一旦你在文章中找到了这些词的位置，使用快速阅读扫描技巧，通过认真阅读相关的句子来找到答案。

The answer is taken directly from the passage. Notice that choices A and B are opposites, so one of them will be incorrect. Look in the text carefully for the exact definition. If you are uncertain, make a table in the margin.

Scan the passage looking for the word you are asked to define. Large or unusual words generally stand out and can be located quickly. Once you have found the position in the passage of the word using quick reading scanning techniques, then focus on the sentence and read carefully.

32. B
句子中提到的是急流和季风是接连发生的。在逐一的观察选项并和文中的内容相比较后，发现选项B是最佳的答案。如果你不确定，可以把文章中的信息先写进表格里。问题的内容是what is the relationship between monsoons and the jet stream.
快速扫描全文并寻找"jet stream"和"monsoon"。

| Tropical Cyclones | Jet Stream |
| Monsoons and Thunderstorms | Different Processes |

The sentences talking about the jet stream and monsoons are next to one another. Trying each definition, and comparing to the text, only choice B fits. If you are uncertain, copy the information from the passage into a table.

The question is, what is the relationship between monsoons and the jet stream.

Scan the passage for "jet stream" and "monsoon."

| Tropical cyclones | Jet stream |
| Monsoons and thunderstorms | Different processes |

33. D
根据文章中的内容逐一的参考每一个选项中的定义，选项D是唯一可以在文中找到相应内容的正确答案。

Referring to the passage, and trying each definition choice, choice D is the only answer that makes sense referring to the text.

34. A
文章中给出的信息是Due to the tilt of the Earth's axis, sunlight reaches the Earth at different angles at different times of the year, creating seasons"。接着替换给出的所有四个选项，你会发现 slanted, 选项A是唯一合理的答案。以下是选项替换后的样子：

a. In June the Northern Hemisphere is slanted towards the sun...

b. In June the Northern Hemisphere is rotating

towards the sun...

c. In June the Northern Hemisphere is connected to towards the sun...

d. In June the Northern Hemisphere is bent towards the sun...

因此选项A是唯一一个合理的选项。

The passage from the text is, "Due to the tilt of the Earth's axis, sunlight reaches the Earth at different angles at different times of the year, creating seasons." Substituting all the choices given into this sentence, slanted, choice A, is the only sensible answer. Here is what substitutions look like:

a. In June the Northern Hemisphere is *slanted* towards the sun...

b. In June the Northern Hemisphere is *rotating* towards the sun...

c. In June the Northern Hemisphere is *connected to* towards the sun...

d. In June the Northern Hemisphere is *bent* towards the sun...

Choice A is the only one that makes sense.

策略10 – 你要认真仔细！细心检查所有的详细依据。

所有的答案都可以通过认真阅读文章来找到。问题内容是对文章中信息的不同方式的描述。

35. C
文章中有很多细节，所以要认真阅读并保持清醒。

The passage has a lot of details so read carefully and stay clear.

36. B
选项设计的目的是为了迷惑考生。阅读文章来找到准确的定义，不要被其他选项所迷惑。

The choices are designed to confuse. Check the text for the exact definition and do not be distracted by other choices.

37. A
这里有一个快速的小诀窍。在选项A中使用了hypovolemic这个词。这是一个不常见的医学类词汇。其他的选项中都没有类似于这样的词汇，所以有很大可能就是正确的答案。你可以快速浏览文章来确认你的答案。在文章中搜索生僻词汇是非常简单和快速的，并且也是这类题目非常有效的答题技巧之一。

Here is a quick tip. On choice A, the word hypovolemic is used. This is an unusual word and specific medical vocabulary. None of the other choices uses any specific vocabulary like this, so it is very likely to be the right answer. You can quickly scan the text for this word to confirm. Scanning the text for an unusual word is easy and fast, and one of the most powerful techniques for this type of question.

38. C
快速浏览文章寻找Zaire这个词。

Scan the text for Zaire.

策略11 - 宏观策略

在回答中心思想和总结性问题的时候，细节可能会对你造成迷惑，但是不要让这些细节使你分心。避开细节部分，使用统揽全文的宏观策略找出正确答案。

39. D
文章中说 "in 2005 it was found there are 3 fruit bat species most suspected of carrying the virus"。其中的细节（三个物种，果蝠和2005年）都不是重要信息。只有bats are suspected是真实信息。

The passage says in 2005 it was found there are 3 fruit bat species most suspected of carrying the virus. The details (3 species, fruit bats and 2005) do not matter. Only the fact that bats are suspected.

40. B
文章中相关的内容是 "Scientists have studied plants, insects and birds as potential reservoir species without success. Bats are the only reservoir species scientists have found."。推断的结果是这些动植物种类不会被感染（例如携带和传播疾病），因此选项B是正确选项。

The relevant passage is, "Scientists have studied plants, insects and birds as potential reservoir species without success. Bats are the only reservoir species scientists have found." The inference is that these plant and animal species cannot be infected, (i.e. carry and transmit the disease) so choice B is correct.

41. A
相关的文章内容是 "Apparently, bats are reservoir species for several viruses"

The relevant passage is,Apparently, bats are reservoir species for several viruses.

策略12

42. D
根据文章内容 "Ebola may not be contagious initially but as the disease progresses, bodily fluids are extremely contagious."，选项B和C是不正确的。选项A在文章中没有任何提及，所以选项D就是正确答案。

Choices B and C are incorrect by the passage, "In the early stages, Ebola may not be highly contagious."Choice A is not mentioned, leaving choice D.

43. B
文章中没有提到任何关于选项A和D的信息。而选项C和题目内容没有任何关系。

Choices A and D are obviously incorrect and can be eliminated right away. Choice C is irrelevant to the question.

44. A
选项B和C在文章中没有提及。选项D可以作为备选项，但是，选项A的内容是包含选项D的并且在文章中有对应的选项。

Choices B and C are not mentioned in the passage. Choice D is a good possibility, however, choice A covers choice D and is referred to in the passage.

45. B
选项A是不正确的。选项C和D在文章中没有提及。

Choice A is incorrect. Choices C and D are not mentioned.

答题卡

阅读理解练习题

Questions 1 - 4 refer to the following passage.

Passage 1: "If You Have Allergies, You're Not Alone"

People who experience allergies might joke that their immune systems have let them down or are seriously lacking. Truthfully though, people who experience allergic reactions or allergy symptoms during certain times of the year have heightened immune systems that are, "better" than those of people who have perfectly healthy but less militant immune systems.

Still, when a person has an allergic reaction, they are having an adverse reaction to a substance that is considered normal to most people. Mild allergic reactions usually have symptoms like itching, runny nose, red eyes, or bumps or discoloration of the skin. More serious allergic reactions, such as those to animal and insect poisons or certain foods, may result in the closing of the throat, swelling of the eyes, low blood pressure, an inability to breathe, and can even be fatal.

Different treatments help different allergies, and which one a person uses depends on the nature and severity of the allergy. It is recommended to patients with severe allergies to take extra precautions, such as carrying an EpiPen, which treats anaphylactic shock and may prevent death, always in order for the remedy to be readily available and more effective. When an allergy is not so severe, treatments may be used just relieve a person of uncomfortable symptoms. Over the counter allergy medicines treat milder symptoms, and can be bought at any grocery store and used in moderation to help people with allergies live normally.

There are many tests available to assess whether a person has allergies or what they may be allergic to, and advances in these tests and the medicine used to treat patients continues to improve. Despite this fact, allergies still affect many people throughout the year or even every day. Medicines used to treat allergies have side effects of their own, and it is difficult to bring the body into balance with the use of medicine. Regardless, many of those who live with allergies are grateful for what is available and find it useful in maintaining their lifestyles.

1. According to this passage, it can be understood that the word "militant" belongs in a group with the words:

    a. sickly, ailing, faint
    b. strength, power, vigor
    c. active, fighting, warring
    d. worn, tired, breaking down

2. The author says that "medicines used to treat allergies have side effects of their own" to

   a. point out that doctors aren't very good at diagnosing and treating allergies

   b. argue that because of the large number of people with allergies, a cure will never be found

   c. explain that allergy medicines aren't cures and some compromise must be made

   d. argue that more wholesome remedies should be researched and medicines banned

3. It can be inferred that _____ recommend that some people with allergies carry medicine with them.

   a. the author

   b. doctors

   c. the makers of EpiPen

   d. people with allergies

4. The author has written this passage to

   a. inform readers on symptoms of allergies so people with allergies can get help

   b. persuade readers to be proud of having allergies

   c. inform readers on different remedies so people with allergies receive the right help

   d. describe different types of allergies, their symptoms, and their remedies

Questions 5 - 8 refer to the following passage.

Passage 2: "When a Poet Longs to Mourn, He Writes an Elegy"

Poems are an expressive, especially emotional, form of writing. They have been present in literature virtually from the time civilizations invented the written word. Poets often portrayed as moody, secluded, and even troubled, but this is because poets are introspective and feel deeply about the current events and cultural norms they are surrounded with. Poets often produce the most telling literature, giving insight into the society and mind-set they come from. This can be done in many forms.

The oldest types of poems often include many stanzas, may or may not rhyme, and are more about telling a story than experimenting with language or words. The most common types of ancient poetry are epics, which are usually extremely long stories that follow a hero through his journey, or elegies, which are often solemn in tone and used to mourn or lament something or someone. The Mesopotamians are often said to have invented the written word, and their literature is among the oldest in the world, including the epic poem titled "Epic of Gilgamesh." Similar in style and length to "Gilgamesh" is "Beowulf," an elegy poem written in Old English and set in Scandinavia. These poems are often used by professors as the earliest examples of literature.

The importance of poetry was revived in the Renaissance. At this time, Europeans discovered the style and beauty of ancient Greek arts, and poetry was among those. Shakespeare is the most well-known poet of the time, and he used poetry not only to write poems but also to write plays for the theater. The most popular forms of poetry during the Renaissance included villanelles (a nineteen-line poem with two rhymes throughout), sonnets, as well as the epic. Poets during this time focused on style and form, and developed very specific rules and outlines for how an exceptional poem should be written.

As often happens in the arts, modern poets have rejected the constricting rules of Renaissance poets, and free form poems are much more popular. Some modern poems would read just like stories if they weren't arranged into lines and stanzas. It is difficult to tell which poems and poets will be the most important, because works of art often become more famous in hindsight, after the poet has died and society can look at itself without being in the moment. Modern poetry continues to develop, and will no doubt continue to change as values, thought, and writing continue to change.

Poems can be among the most enlightening and uplifting texts for a person to read if they are looking to connect with the past, connect with other people, or try to gain an understanding of what is happening in their time.

5. In summary, the author has written this passage

a. as a foreword that will introduce a poem in a book or magazine

b. because she loves poetry and wants more people to like it

c. to give a brief history of poems

d. to convince students to write poems

6. The author organizes the paragraphs mainly by

a. moving chronologically, explaining which types of poetry were common in that time

b. talking about new types of poems each paragraph and explaining them a little

c. focusing on one poet or group of people and the poems they wrote

d. explaining older types of poetry so she can talk about modern poetry

7. The author's claim that poetry has been around "virtually from the time civilizations invented the written word" is supported by the detail that

a. Beowulf is written in Old English, which is not really in use any longer

b. epic poems told stories about heroes

c. the Renaissance poets tried to copy Greek poets

d. the Mesopotamians are credited with both inventing the word and writing "Epic of Gilgamesh"

8. According to the passage, it can be understood that the word "telling" means

    a. speaking
    b. significant
    c. soothing
    d. wordy

Questions 9 - 12 refer to the following passage.

Passage 3: "Winged Victory of Samothrace: the Statue of the Gods"

Students who read about the "Winged Victory of Samothrace" probably won't be able to picture what this statue looks like. However, almost anyone who knows a little about statues will recognize it when they see it: it is the statue of a winged woman who does not have arms or a head. Even the most famous pieces of art may be recognized by sight but not by name.

This iconic statue is of the Greek goddess Nike, who represented victory and was called Victoria by the Romans. The statue is sometimes called the "Nike of Samothrace." She was often displayed in Greek art as driving a chariot, and her speed or efficiency with the chariot may be what her wings symbolize. It is said that the statue was created around 200 BCE to celebrate a battle that was won at sea. Archaeologists and art historians believe the statue may have originally been part of a temple or other building, even one of the most important temples, Megaloi Theoi, just as many statues were used during that time.

"Winged Victory" does indeed appear to have had arms and a head when it was originally created, and it is unclear why they were removed or lost. Indeed, they have never been discovered, even with all the excavation that has taken place. Many speculate that one of her arms was raised and put to her mouth, as though she was shouting or calling out, which is consistent with the idea of her as a war figure. If the missing pieces were ever to be found, they might give Greek and art historians more of an idea of what Nike represented or how the statue was used. Learning about pieces of art through details like these can help students remember time frames or locations, as well as learn about the people who occupied them.

9. The author's title says the statue is "of the Gods" because

    a. the statue is very beautiful and even a god would find it beautiful

    b. the statue is of a Greek goddess, and gods were of primary importance to the Greek

    c. Nike lead the gods into war

    d. the statues were used at the temple of the gods and so it belonged to them

10. The third paragraph states that

   a. the statue is related to war and was probably broken apart by foreign soldiers

   b. the arms and head of the statue cannot be found because all the excavation has taken place

   c. speculations have been made about what the entire statue looked like and what it symbolized

   d. the statue has no arms or head because the sculptor lost them

11. The author's main purpose in writing this passage is to

   a. demonstrate that art and culture are related and one can teach us about the other

   b. persuade readers to become archeologists and find the missing pieces of the statue

   c. teach readers about the Greek goddess Nike

   d. to teach readers the name of a statue they probably recognize

12. The author specifies the indirect audience as "students" because

   a. it is probably a student who is taking this test

   b. most young people don't know much about art yet and most young people are students

   c. students read more than people who are not students

   d. the passage is based on a discussion of what we can learn about culture from art

Questions 13 - 16 refer to the following passage.

Passage 4: "Ways Characters Communicate in Theater"

Playwrights give their characters voices in a way that gives depth and added meaning to what happens on stage during their play. There are different types of speech in scripts that allow characters to talk with themselves, with other characters, and even with the audience.

It is very unique to theater that characters may talk "to themselves." When characters do this, the speech they give is called a soliloquy. Soliloquies are usually poetic, introspective, moving, and can tell audience members about the feelings, motivations, or suspicions of an individual character without that character having to reveal them to other characters on stage. "To be or not to be" is a famous soliloquy given by Hamlet as he considers difficult but important themes, such as life and death.

The most common type of communication in plays is when one character is speaking to another or a group of other characters. This is generally called dialogue, but can also be called monologue if one character speaks without being interrupted for a long time. It is not necessarily the most important type of communication, but it is the most common because the plot of the play cannot really progress without it.

Lastly, and most unique to theater (although it has been used somewhat in film) is when a character speaks directly to the audience. This is called an aside, and scripts usually specifically direct actors to do this. Asides are usually comical, an inside joke between the character and the audience, and very short. The actor will usually face the audience when delivering them, even if it's for a moment, so the audience can recognize this move as an aside.

All three of these types of communication are important to the art of theater, and have been perfected by famous playwrights like Shakespeare. Understanding these types of communication can help an audience member grasp what is artful about the script and action of a play.

13. According to the passage, characters in plays communicate to

    a. move the plot forward

    b. show the private thoughts and feelings of one character

    c. make the audience laugh

    d. add beauty and artistry to the play

14. When Hamlet delivers "To be or not to be," he can most likely be described as

    a. solitary

    b. thoughtful

    c. dramatic

    d. hopeless

15. The author uses parentheses to punctuate "although it has been used somewhat in film"

    a. to show that films are less important

    b. instead of using commas so that the sentence is not interrupted

    c. because parenthesis help separate details that are not as important

    d. to show that films are not as artistic

16. It can be understood that by the phrase "give their characters voices," the author means that

    a. playwrights are generous

    b. playwrights are changing the sound or meaning of characters' voices to fit what they had in mind

    c. dialogue is important in creating characters

    d. playwrights may be the parent of one of their actors and literally give them their voice

Questions 17 - 20 refer to the following passage.

Passage 5: "Women and Advertising"

Only in the last few generations have media messages been so widespread and so readily seen, heard, and read by so many people. Advertising is an important part of both selling and buying anything from soap to cereal to jeans. For whatever reason, more consumers are women than are men. Media message are subtle but powerful, and more attention has been paid lately to how these message affect women.

Of all the products that women buy, makeup, clothes, and other stylistic or cosmetic products are among the most popular. This means that companies focus their advertising on women, promising them that their product will make her feel, look, or smell better than the next company's product will. This competition has resulted in advertising that is more and more ideal and less and less possible for everyday women. However, because women do look to these ideals and the products they represent as how they can potentially become, many women have developed unhealthy attitudes about themselves when they have failed to become those ideals.

In recent years, more companies have tried to change advertisements to be healthier for women. This includes featuring models of more sizes and addressing a huge outcry against unfair tools such as airbrushing and photo editing. There is debate about what the right balance between real and ideal is, because fashion is also considered art and some changes are made to purposefully elevate fashionable products and signify that they are creative, innovative, and the work of individual people. Artists want their freedom protected as much as women do, and advertising agencies are often caught in the middle.

Some claim that the companies who make these changes are not doing enough. Many people worry that there are still not enough models of different sizes and different ethnicities. Some people claim that companies use this healthier type of advertisement not for the good of women, but because they would like to sell products to the women who are looking for these kinds of messages. This is also a hard balance to find: companies do need to make money, and women do need to feel respected.

While the focus of this change has been on women, advertising can also affect men, and this change will hopefully be a lesson on media for all consumers.

17. The second paragraph states that advertising focuses on women

  a. to shape what the ideal should be

  b. because women buy makeup

  c. because women are easily persuaded

  d. because of the types of products that women buy

18. According to the passage, fashion artists and female consumers are at odds because

  a. there is a debate going on and disagreement drives people apart

  b. both of them are trying to protect their freedom to do something

  c. artists want to elevate their products above the reach of women

  d. women are creative, innovative, individual people

19. The author uses the phrase "for whatever reason" in this passage to

   a. keep the focus of the paragraph on media messages and not on the differences between men and women

   b. show that the reason for this is unimportant

   c. argue that it is stupid that more women are consumers than men

   d. show that he or she is tired of talking about why media messages are important

20. This passage suggests that

   a. advertising companies are still working on making their messages better

   b. all advertising companies seek to be more approachable for women

   c. women are only buying from companies that respect them

   d. artists could stop producing fashionable products if they feel bullied

Questions 21 - 24 refer to the following passage.

Passage 6: "FDR, the Treaty of Versailles, and the Fourteen Points"

At the conclusion of World War I, both who had won the war and those who were forced to admit defeat welcomed the end of the war and anticipated that a peace treaty would be signed. The American president, Franklin Roosevelt, played an important part in proposing what the agreements should be and did so through his Fourteen Points.

World War I had begun in 1914 when an Austrian archduke was assassinated, leading to a domino effect that pulled the world's most powerful countries into war on a large scale. The war catalyzed the creation and use of deadly weapons that had not previously existed, resulting in a great loss of soldiers on both sides of the fighting. More than 9 million soldiers were killed.

The United States agreed to enter the war right before it ended, and they believed that its decision to become finally involved brought on the end of the war. FDR made it very clear that the U.S. was entering the war for moral reasons and had an agenda focused on world peace. The Fourteen Points were individual goals and ideas (focused on peace, free trade, open communication, and self reliance) that FDR wanted the power nations to strive for now that the war had concluded. He was optimistic and had many ideas about what could be accomplished through and during the post-war peace. However, FDR's fourteen points were poorly received when he presented them to the leaders of other world powers, many of whom wanted only to help their own countries and to punish the Germans for fueling the war, and they fell by the wayside. World War II was imminent, for Germany lost everything.

Some historians believe that the other leaders who participated in the Treaty of Versailles weren't receptive to the Fourteen Points because World War I was fought almost entirely on European soil, and the United States lost much less than did the other powers. FDR was in a unique position to help determine the fate of the war, but doing it on his own terms did not help accomplish his goals. This is only one historical example of how the United State has tried to use its power as an important country, but found itself limited because of geological or ideological factors.

21. The main idea of this passage is that

a. World War I was unfair because no fighting took place in America

b. World War II happened because of the Treaty of Versailles

c. the power the United States has to help other countries also prevents it from helping other countries

d. Franklin Roosevelt was one of the United States' smartest presidents

22. According to the second paragraph, World War I started because

a. an archduke was assassinated

b. weapons that were more deadly had been developed

c. a domino effect of allies agreeing to help

d. the world's most powerful countries were large

23. The author includes the detail that 9 million soldiers were killed

a. to demonstrate why European leaders were hesitant to accept peace

b. to show the reader the dangers of deadly weapons

c. to make the reader think about which countries lost the most soldiers

d. to demonstrate why World War II was imminent

24. According to this passage, it can be understood that the word catalyzed means

a. analyzed

b. sped up

c. invented

d. funded

应答键

文章1: "If You Have Allergies, You're Not Alone"

1. C
这个问题考察的是读者的词汇能力。否定词 "but" 和 "less" 的使用，特别是接连的使用，可能会导致读者选择A或者D，这两个都是 "militant" 的反义词。读者通过对比健康的人和极度健康的人可能会产生迷惑 – 两者都是健康的，但是读者在对比中可能会寻找出哪一个比较 "worse"，因此错误的选择了反义词。理解 "militant" 的关键是，如果读者不熟悉这个单词，要去寻找这个词的词根；利用词根，读者可以很轻松的与 "military" 进行关联并且能得到这个词想表达的意思：防御（特别指在免疫系统中的身体抵抗）。与选项B相比，选项C是正确的，因为 "militant" 是一个形容词，与选项C中的词性相同，而选项B是名词。

This question tests the reader's vocabulary skills. The uses of the negatives "but" and "less," especially right next to each other, may confuse readers into answering with choices A or D, which list words that are antonyms of "militant." Readers may also be confused by the comparison of healthy people with what is being described as an overly healthy person--both people are good, but the reader may look for which one is "worse" in the comparison, and therefore stray toward the antonyms. One key to understanding the meaning of "militant" if the reader is unfamiliar with it is to look at the root of the word; readers can then easily associate it with "military" and gain a sense of what the word signifies: defense (especially considered that the immune system defends the body). Choice C is correct over choice B because "militant" is an adjective, just as the words in C are, whereas the words in B are nouns.

2. C
这个问题考察的是读者对写作功能性的理解能力。其他选项的内容都是围绕着引用内容的具体细节，可能会对读者造成迷惑。选项A在某种程度上与文章之前的内容相悖，也就是测试和治疗在进步，也许医生也会和它们一同进步，但是文章中完全没有提及到医生，并且问题的中心是药品。对于不细心的读者来说，选项B看似是正确的，当作者提及到大量受影响的群体时，他突出指出的是现实中长期受过敏困扰的人群，而不是治疗各种过敏的可能性。同样的，当作者提到身体的"balance"，很容易联想到"wholesome"，但是作者实际上并没有争论或者下结论说抗过敏药物应当被全面禁止。并且，因为这篇文章的主旨是说过敏与生活的共存，因此选项C是相对于题目和文章内容最恰当的选项。

This question tests the reader's understanding of function within writing. The other choices are details included surrounding the quoted text, and may therefore confuse the reader. A somewhat contradicts what is said earlier in the paragraph, which is that tests and treatments are improving, and probably doctors are along with them, but the paragraph doesn't actually mention doctors, and the subject of the question is the medicine. Choice B may seem correct to readers who aren't careful to understand that, while the author does mention the large number of people affected, the author is touching on the realities of living with allergies rather about the likelihood of curing all allergies. Similarly, while the author does mention the "balance" of the body, which is easily associated with "wholesome," the author is not really making an argument and especially is not making an extreme statement that allergy medicines should be outlawed. Again, because the article's tone is on living with allergies, choice C is an appropriate choice that fits with the title and content of the text.

3. B

这道题考察的是读者的推理能力。文章中并没有说谁在给出建议，但是通过"patients"的使用以及文章的大致内容，可以根据逻辑推理出选项B"doctors"。作者在文中提到了建议，但并不是通过直接的方式（例如"I recommend that"），所以选项A可以被删除掉。选项D看似是正确的，因为患有过敏疾病的人可以为其他过敏患者提供药品或产品的建议，但是文章中并没有支持相关内容的具体信息。选项C也可能是正确的，因为当中特别提到了EpiPen，但是介绍它的时候用到了词组"such as"，因此不足以证明建议是来自它的发明者。

This question tests the reader's inference skills. The text does not state who is doing the recommending, but the use of the "patients," as well as the general context of the passage, lends itself to the logical partner, "doctors," B. The author does mention the recommendation but doesn't present it as her own (i.e. "I recommend that"), so A may be eliminated. It may seem plausible that people with allergies (D) may recommend medicines or products to other people with allergies, but the text does not necessarily support this interaction taking place. Choice C may be selected because the EpiPen is specifically mentioned, but the use of the phrase "such as" when it is introduced is not limiting enough to assume the recommendation is coming from its creators.

4. D

这个问题考察的是读者对全文的统揽理解能力。选项D包含了三个段落的中心思想，但是这个选项并没有像其他三个选项一样，针对三段内容的任何一方面或者某一段文章内容，而是片面的给出了一个作者想传达的意思。由于文章的题目和"better"这个词的使用，读者还有可能选择B，但是文章想传达的是比这个词更大更整体的信息。

This question tests the reader's global understanding of the text. Choice D includes the main topics of the three body paragraphs, and isn't too focused on a specific aspect or quote from the text, as the other questions are, giving a skewed summary of what the author intended. The reader may be drawn to Choice B because of the title of the passage and the use of words like "better," but the message of the passage is larger and more general than this.

文章2："When a Poet Longs to Mourn, He Writes an Elegy"

5. C
这道题考察的是读者的概括能力。"actually"这个词的使用，在描述诗人是什么样的人时，以及其他类似的情况中，都有可能会引导读者去选择选项B或者D，但是实际上作者给出了更多支持的信息，而不是去劝说读者。读者没有给出任何指示说她喜爱诗歌（B）或者人们，特别是学生（D），需要写诗。选项A是不正确的，因为其中的类型和内容与序言的内容不符；序言通常会根据强调特定的诗歌的历史背景和概念，来充分介绍诗的内容并且来凸显与其他诗歌的不同。这里作者根据几首诗给出了概括性的陈述。不同的是，她讲述了几个关于这几首诗的故事，如同选项C所述，通过给出三段时间背景来对诗歌的历史做了概括性的描述。

This question tests the reader's summarization skills. The use of the word "actually" in describing what kind of people poets are, as well as other moments like this, may lead readers to selecting choice B or D, but the author is more information than trying to persuade readers. The author gives no indication that she loves poetry (B) or that people, students specifically (D), should write poems. Choice A is incorrect because the style and content of this paragraph do not match those of a foreword; forewords usually focus on the history or ideas of a specific poem to introduce it more fully and help it stand out against other poems. The author here focuses on several poems and gives broad statements. Instead, she tells a kind of story about poems, giving three very broad time periods in which to discuss them, thereby giving a brief history of poetry, as choice C states.

6. A

这个问题考察的是读者的概括能力。每段中心句的关键词("oldest","Renaissance","modern")可以告诉读者文章是按照时间顺序进行写作的。段落中的起始和结尾句都是总结概括性的陈述。选项B看似是合理的，但是由于两段中都提到了史诗，所以在每段中都使用了新类型的诗歌这个概念是错误的。选项C也可以被排除掉因为作者清楚的说到几种不同的诗人，派别和诗歌的类型。作者所写的内容从旧时期向新时期转变，从这个角度看，选项D看似是正确的，但是"so(that)"的使用使这个选项变成错误的，因为作者在文中没有任何内容表示出她很匆忙（每一段的长度都差不多）或者她更倾向于现代诗歌。

This question tests the reader's summarization skills. Key words in the topic sentences of each of the paragraphs ("oldest," "Renaissance," "modern") should give the reader an idea that the author is moving chronologically. The opening and closing sentence-paragraphs are broad and talk generally. Choice B seems reasonable, but epic poems are mentioned in two paragraphs, eliminating the idea that only new types of poems are used in each paragraph. Choice C is also easily eliminated because the author clearly mentions several different poets, groups of people, and poems. Choice D also seems reasonable, considering that the author does move from older forms of poetry to newer forms, but use of "so (that)" makes this statement false, for the author gives no indication that she is rushing (the paragraphs are about the same size) or that she prefers modern poetry.

7. D
这个问题考察的是读者对细节的观察能力。其中的关键词是"invented"- 它与Mesopotamians相连，这些人创造了文字，并且作为先驱，他们还发明使用了诗歌。其他几个选项针对了文章中不同的细节内容，例如Renaissance's admiration of the Greeks (C) and that Beowulf is in Old English (A)。选项B看上去是一个吸引人的选项，因为英雄的概念在古代和早期的文明时期是根深蒂固的。

This question tests the reader's attention to detail. The key word is "invented"--it ties together the Mesopotamians, who invented the written word, and the fact that they, as the inventors, also invented and used poetry. The other selections focus on other details mentioned in the passage, such as that the Renaissance's admiration of the Greeks (C) and that Beowulf is in Old English (A). Choice B may seem like an attractive answer because it is unlike the others and because the idea of heroes seems rooted in ancient and early civilizations.

8. B
这道题考察的是读者的词汇量和语境分析的能力。"Telling"是一个很普通的词，但是在这里的使用可能是一个读者不熟悉的方法，在这里它是一个形容词而不是通常的动名词形式。如果读者按照通常的方法来选择动词，那选项A就是一个明显正确的答案。但是如果读者知道这个词是以形容词的方式出现，那么就会避开选项A这个陷阱而选择选项D "wordy"，但是这个词和文章内容不符。选项C可以很容易被排除掉，因为它和文章或段落中的任何内容都没有联系。"Significant"（B）与文章的内容一致，特别是与后面句子中"give insight"这个词组有直接关系。

This question tests the reader's vocabulary and contextualization skills. "Telling" is not an unusual word, but it may be used here in a way that is not familiar to readers, as an adjective rather than a verb in gerund form. Choice A may seem like the obvious answer to a reader looking for a verb to match the use they are familiar with. If the reader understands that the word is being used as an adjective and that choice A is a ploy, they may opt to select choice D, "wordy," but it does not make sense in context. Choice C can be easily eliminated, and doesn't have any connection to the paragraph or passage. "Significant" (B) does make sense contextually, especially relative to the phrase "give insight" used later in the sentence.

文章3："Winged Victory of Samothrace: the Statue of the Gods"

9. B
这个问题考察的是读者的概括能力。选项A是一个概括性的陈述，可能正确也可能不正确，它看似与上下文内容相符，但是和文章内容没有直接的联系。作者提到神殿中的雕塑可能是为了祭奠Greek Gods（D），但是并没有讨论或者争论众神对于神殿或者其龙头的态度。选项C指出了Nike引发了众神之间的一场战争（泰坦之战），但是文章中并没有与其相关的内容，对这个背景有了解的学生可能会因为没有认真全面的分析文章中的具体内容而误选这个选项。选项B是一个非常恰当的描述，把强调的重点与文章主旨联系了起来，也就是希腊神对于希腊文化的重要性。

This question tests the reader's summarization skills. Choice A is a very broad statement that may or may not be true, and seems to be in context, but has nothing to do with the passage. The author does mention that the statue was probably used on a temple dedicated to the Greek gods (D), but in no way discusses or argues for the gods' attitude toward or claim on these temples or its faucets. Nike does indeed lead the gods into a war (the Titan war), as choice C suggests, but this is not mentioned by the passage and students who know this may be drawn to this answer but have not done a close enough analysis of the text that is actually in the passage. Choice B is appropriately expository, and connects the titular emphasis to the idea that the Greek gods are very important to Greek culture.

10. C

这个问题考察的是读者的概括能力。选项C是将文章的内容直接从段落中截取出来，但并不是一字不差的摘抄，所以看起来很明显是正确答案。正如选项A说明的一样，文章中谈及到Nike是战争女神，但是这一内容在第三段中只是轻描淡写，并且推理出战士们摧毁了雕像，然而题目问的是第三段中着重描述了什么内容。选项B也是直接从文中截取的内容，但是进行了一个小而重要的改变：选项中"all"和"never"的使用太具有局限性，而文中并没有提及这些局限。如果读者选择了选项D，会因为自我推理而造成对此类问题的错误引导。段落中只提到了手臂和头部的"lost"而并没有指出是谁造成它们的丢失。

This question tests the reader's summarization skills. The test for question choice C is pulled straight from the paragraph, but is not word-for-word, so it may seem too obvious to be the right answer. The passage does talk about Nike being the goddess of war, as choice A states, but the third paragraph only touches on it and it is an inference that soldiers destroyed the statue, when this question is asking specifically for what the third paragraph actually stated. Choice B is also straight from the text, with a minor but key change: the inclusion of the words "all" and "never" are too limiting and the passage does not suggest that these limits exist. If a reader selects choice D, they are also making an inference that is misguided for this type of question. The paragraph does state that the arms and head are "lost" but does not suggest who lost them.

11. A
这个问题考察的是读者区分写作功能的能力。根据段落的具有说明性而不是说服性的目的，选项B可以被排除。不论作者是否发觉，文章内容都没有任何争论性的目的。选项C和D都可以在段落中找到相应的细节，但是两者都不是围绕着整个文章内容说明的，文章的主旨是说，如果从艺术中进行文化的学习并且对两个之间的关联性进行推测，因此建议选择选项A。

This question tests the reader's ability to recognize function in writing. Choice B can be eliminated based on the purpose of the passage, which is expository and not persuasive. The author may or may not feel this way, but the passage does not show evidence of being argumentative for that purpose. Choices C and D are both details found in the text, but neither of them encompasses the entire message of the passage, which has an overall message of learning about culture from art and making guesses about how the two are related, as suggested by choice A.

12. D
这个问题考察的是读者对字里行间的理解能力。大多数的备选项都是概括性的描述，可能正确也可能是错误的。It probably is a student who is taking the test on which

this question is featured (A)，但是作者没有针对参加考试的人，也没有以测试的形式同观众进行对话。同样的，由于学校和成绩的原因，students read more than adults (C) 这个陈述也可能是正确的，但是只看第一句话中动词"read"太具有局限性，而错过了这个文章向表达的大范围的意思；并且利用相同的方法来排出选项B。当所有的陈述都正确的情况下，选项D是最贴切的答案，它正确的推断出文章想表达的目的，并且没有做出任何错误的假设。

This question tests the reader's ability to understand function within writing. Most of the possible selections are very general statements which may or may not be true. It probably is a student who is taking the test on which this question is featured (A), but the author makes no address to the test taker and is not talking to the audience in terms of the test. Likewise, it may also be true that students read more than adults (C), mandated by schools and grades, but the focus on the verb "read" in the first sentence is too narrow and misses the larger purpose of the passage; the same could be said for selection B. While all the statements could be true, choice D is the most germane, and infers the purpose of the passage without making assumptions that could be incorrect.

文章4: "Ways Characters Communicate in Theater"

13. D

这个问题考察的是读者的概括能力。问题问的是关于这个文章的概括性的内容，而文章的标题"Ways Characters Communicate in Theater"给出了明确的指示。A，B，C其他三个选项都是与文中直接相关的内容，因此读者可能会误选它们其中的一个，但是它们的内容都因太过具体而压缩了这个文章的内容及它所想传达的信息。

This question tests the reader's summarization

skills. The question is asking very generally about the message of the passage, and the title, "Ways Characters Communicate in Theater," is one indication of that. The other choices A, B, and C are all directly from the text, and therefore readers may be inclined to select one of them, but are too specific to encapsulate the entirety of the passage and its message.

14. B
独白的那段内容提到了"To be or not to be",这是文章中的原文,读者可能会因为"To be or not to be"是哈姆雷特的一句独白而猜测他在表述这句话的时候正在自我反省或者深刻思考。演员在独白的时候可能会传达"solitary"(A)的意思,但是"thoughtful"(B)是对于文章整体大意的更正确的选项。读者可能会选择选项C,因为戏剧和剧场可以是互换使用的,并且文章提及到了独白是剧场独有的(因此也是戏剧独有的),但是这个答案对于问题段落不够准确。读者也有可能通过生与死的主题以及哈姆雷特的意图去选择he is"hopeless"(D),但是这些主题在段落和文章中都没有提及过,通过对文章认真的分析阅读可以得到印证。

The paragraph on soliloquies mentions "To be or not to be," and it is from the context of that paragraph that readers may understand that because "To be or not to be" is a soliloquy, Hamlet will be introspective, or thoughtful, while delivering it. It is true that actors deliver soliloquies alone, and may be "solitary" (A), but "thoughtful" (B) is more true to the overall idea of the paragraph. Readers may choose C because drama and theater can be used interchangeably and the passage mentions that soliloquies are unique to theater (and therefore drama), but this answer is not specific enough to the paragraph in question. Readers may pick up on the theme of life and death and Hamlet's true intentions and select that he is "hopeless" (D), but those themes are not discussed either by this paragraph or passage, as a close textual reading and analysis confirms.

15. C
这个问题考察的是读者的语法能力。选项B看似是正确的，但是插入语的使用比逗号更能起到分割句子的作用，具体到本题的句子来说，实际上破坏了句子的结构。选项A和D将剧场和电影之间做了对比，然而文章中并没有，因此可能是正确也可能是错误的。这个细节，通过添加it is not completely unique to theater 这个描述来表明，旁白是剧场里独有的内容，这也可能是作者没有删除它的原因，而是使用插入语来表明细节的重要性（C）。

This question tests the reader's grammatical skills. Choice B seems logical, but parenthesis are actually considered to be a stronger break in a sentence than commas are, and along this line of thinking, actually disrupt the sentence more. Choices A and D make comparisons between theater and film that are simply not made in the passage, and may or may not be true. This detail does clarify the statement that asides are most unique to theater by adding that it is not completely unique to theater, which may have been why the author didn't chose not to delete it and instead used parentheses to designate the detail's importance (C).

16. C
这个问题考察的是读者的词汇以及对语境把握的能力。选项A有可能是正确的，但是它错误的强调了"give"这个词的作用并且忽视了与文章紧密相关的句子后面的内容。如果读者过多的依赖于"give"这个词，有可能会选择选项B和D，但是选项C中单词的抽象意义才是需要抓住的信息点，并且这个选项也准确恰当的描述了整个文章内容。
This question tests the reader's vocabulary and

contextualization skills. Choice A may or may not be true, but focuses on the wrong function of the word "give" and ignores the rest of the sentence, which is more relevant to what the passage is discussing. Choices B and D may also be selected if the reader depends too literally on the word "give," failing to grasp the more abstract function of the word that is the focus of choice C, which also properly acknowledges the entirety of the passage and its meaning.

文章 5: "Women and Advertising"

17. D
这个问题考察的是读者的概括能力。其他三个选项A，B和C着重描述了第二段的部分内容，描述的过于具体而且和问题中的内容无关。句子的复杂性可能导致学生会错误的选择这三个选项中的一个，但是重新组合句子或者对句子的转述可以帮助答题者寻找出正确的答案。除此之外，选项A对公司的意图做了一个没有确定性的假设，选项B强调了其中一个产品而不是研发产品的创意，选项C做出了对女性的一个没有确定性的假设并且在文章中没有相应的内容支持。

This question tests the reader's summarization skills. The other choices A, B, and C focus on portions of the second paragraph that are too narrow and do not relate to the specific portion of text in question. The complexity of the sentence may mislead students into selecting one of these answers, but rearranging or restating the sentence will lead the reader to the correct answer. In addition, choice A makes an assumption that may or may not be true about the intentions of the company, choice B focuses on one product rather than the idea of the products, and choice C makes an assumption about women that may or may not be true and is not supported by the text.

18. B

这个问题考察的是读者对细节的观察能力。如果读者选择A，是因为他们选择了"debate"这个词的定义，并且非常有逻辑的假设了两者之间是因为彼此冲突而不一致的；然而，在文章中并没有相应的支持信息。选项C也截取了文章中的一段内容，但是对内容作了一些改动并表达了错误的意思。艺术家们想令他们的创意凌驾于其他艺术家的创意之上，因此表现出他们是"creative"和"innovative"的。同样的，选项D截取了文章中一部分内容，但是对其做了修改并传达了干扰信息。文章中描述的是艺术家希望成为"creative, innovative, individual people"而不是女性。

This question tests reader's attention to detail. If a reader selects A, he or she may have picked up on the use of the word "debate" and assumed, very logically, that the two are at odds because they are fighting; however, this is simply not supported in the text. Choice C also uses very specific quotes from the text, but it rearranges them and gives them false meaning. The artists want to elevate their creations above the creations of other artists, thereby showing that they are "creative" and "innovative." Similarly, choice D takes phrases straight from the texts and rearranges and confuses them. The artists are described as wanting to be "creative, innovative, individual people," not the women.

19. A

这个问题考察的是读者的词汇和概括能力。如果读者把注意力集中在"whatever"这个词上，有可能会认为作者对题目中的这个词的使用是草率而不加考虑的，因此会根据它通常和会话的意思对这道题做出错误的判断。这样，读者可能会错误的选择选项B和C，因为他们之中分别包含"unimportant"和"stupid"这两个词。选项D也是一个类似的误导选项，全文描述的是media的信息，而当题目中的这个词出现在文章的开头时是不符合文章大意的。选项A在文字上和上下文中都是恰当的，读者可以清楚了解作者希望在开头段中集中表现后面文章所想讨论的内容。

This question tests reader's vocabulary and summarization skills. This phrase, used by the author, may seem flippant and dismissive if readers focus on the word "whatever" and misinterpret it as a popular, colloquial terms. In this way, the choices B and C may mislead the reader to selecting one of them by including the terms "unimportant" and "stupid," respectively. Choice D is a similar misreading, but doesn't make sense when the phrase is at the beginning of the passage and the entire passage is on media messages. Choice A is literarily and contextually appropriate, and the reader can understand that the author would like to keep the introduction focused on the topic the passage is going to discuss.

20. A

这个题考察的是读者的推理能力。选项B中"all"这个词的极端使用表明了每一个广告公司 are working to be approachable，但是这看起来并不是正确的，而且文章中明确的指出了"more" companies have done this，虽然表明了未来的某一天他们都会参加的可能性，但是就现在来说，他们之中不是所有公司都参加。选项C中限定词"only"的使用也导致了相同的问题；女性们仍然会从那些不在意这则消息的商家购买，或者那些已经歇业的商家，但是文中特别指出了"many" women are worried about media messages，而不是所有。读者可能会发现选项D是符合逻辑的，特别是在他们试图做出推理的时候，虽然是有正确的可能性，但是在文章中并没有建议和讨论过这件事。选项A是正确的，因为选项中"still working"和文中"will hopefully"以及对于公司困境的大量讨论之间的关系，文章中表明了这还是一个需要时间来完成的事情。

This question tests a reader's inference skills. The extreme use of the word "all" in choice B suggests that every single advertising company are working to be approachable, and while this is not only unlikely, the text specifically states that "more" companies have done this, signifying that they have not all participated, even if it's a possibility that they may some day. The use of the limiting word "only" in choice C lends that answer similar problems; women are still buying from companies who do not care about this message, or those companies would not be in business, and the passage specifies that "many" women are worried about media messages, but not all. Readers may find choice D logical, especially if they are looking to make an inference, and while this may be a possibility, the passage does not suggest or discuss this happening. Choice A is correct based on specifically because of the relation between "still working" in the answer and "will hopefully" and the extensive discussion on companies struggles, which come only with progress, in the text.

文章 6: "FDR, the Treaty of Versailles, and the Fourteen Points"

21. C

这个问题考察的是读者的概述能力。这篇文章的中心思想是，在其他国家损失惨重的情况下，美国总统也许没有足够的根据来支持他的十四点原则。选项A是根据文章直接推断出来的，但是并没有表达整篇文章所要想传达的信息。选项B也是根据文章推导出来的，选项中说战争是"imminent"，但是也没有表达整个文章的观点。整篇文章看上去并没有称赞FDR，或者至少有尊敬他的态度，文章既没有从任何角度说明他是最具智慧的总统，也没有表明这是其他人的观点。选项C是一个明显的正确答案，它直接和文章内容相关并将原句做了转述。

This question tests the reader's summarization skills. The entire passage is leading up to the idea that the president of the US may not have had grounds to assert his Fourteen Points when other countries had lost so much. Choice A is pretty directly inferred by the text, but it does not adequately summarize what the entire passage is trying to communicate. Choice B may also be inferred by the passage when it says that the war is "imminent," but it does not represent the entire message, either. The passage does seem to be in praise of FDR, or at least in respect of him, but it does not in any way claim that he is the smartest president, nor does this represent the many other points included. Choice C is then the obvious answer, and most directly relates to the closing sentences which it rewords.

22. C
这个题目考察的是学生对细节的观察能力。选项A和B都是正确的描述，因为在文中都有相应的对照，它们都很相似的解释了战争开始的原因，但是这两个都不是文章中给出的真正的原因。选项D错误的使用了文章中的词义，指出了战争中最强大的国家而不是引发战争的原因。正如正确选项C描述的一样，文章中直接表明了是多米诺效应引发了战争。

This question tests the reader's attention to detail. The passage does state that choices A and B are true, and while those statements are in proximity to the explanation for why the war started, they are not the actual reason given. Choice D is a mix up of words used in the passage, which says that the largest powers were in play but not that this fact somehow started the war. The passage does make a direct statement that a domino effect started the war, supporting choice C as the correct answer.

23. A

这道题考察的是读者对写作功能的理解能力。整篇文章描述的是，因为对战争的不满以及在战争中极其惨重的损失，其他各国的领导人对于是否接受宽宏或者和平的条约是持犹豫态度的。文章中提及到了具有毁灭性的杀伤力武器（B），虽然这个真实的，带有情感的内容的使用具有极大的目的性，但是武器并不是整篇文章的主旨。因为文章中提到了有多个国家参加以及各国不同程度的损失，读者可能会考虑哪个国家损失的战士数量最多（C），但是这部分内容在文中并没有涉及。选项D和选项A是相关的，但是选项A更直接和具体的描述了文章中的内容。

This question tests the reader's understanding of functions in writing. Throughout the passage, it states that leaders of other nations were hesitant to accept generous or peaceful terms because of the grievances of the war, and the great loss of life was chief among these. While the passage does touch on the devastation of deadly weapons (B), the use of this raw, emotional fact serves a much larger purpose, and the focus of the passage is not the weapons. While readers may indeed consider who lost the most soldiers (C) when so many countries were involved and the inequalities of loss are mentioned in the passage, there is no discussion of this in the passage. Choice D is related to A, but choice A is more direct and relates more to the passage.

24. B

这个问题考察的是读者的词汇能力。选项A看上去是一个吸引读者的选项，因为它在语言学上与"catalyzed"相似，但是在字义上两者并没有什么关系。选项C与文章内容相符，但是放入句子中会造成内容的重复而不符合逻辑。即使读者可能认为资金的使用是用于生产更多的武器，特别是高级武器，选项D也与上下文内容不符。

This question tests the reader's vocabulary skills.

Choice A may seem appealing to readers because it is phonetically similar to "catalyzed," but the two are not related in any other way. Choice C makes sense in context, but if plugged into the sentence creates a redundancy that doesn't make sense. Choice D does also not make sense contextually, even if the reader may consider that funds were needed to create more weaponry, especially if it was advanced.

听力

答题卡

	A	B	C	D	E		A	B	C	D	E
1	○	○	○	○	○	21	○	○	○	○	○
2	○	○	○	○	○	22	○	○	○	○	○
3	○	○	○	○	○	23	○	○	○	○	○
4	○	○	○	○	○	24	○	○	○	○	○
5	○	○	○	○	○	25	○	○	○	○	○
6	○	○	○	○	○						
7	○	○	○	○	○						
8	○	○	○	○	○						
9	○	○	○	○	○						
10	○	○	○	○	○						
11	○	○	○	○	○						
12	○	○	○	○	○						
13	○	○	○	○	○						
14	○	○	○	○	○						
15	○	○	○	○	○						
16	○	○	○	○	○						
17	○	○	○	○	○						
18	○	○	○	○	○						
19	○	○	○	○	○						
20	○	○	○	○	○						

方法： 使用智能手机或者平板电脑扫描下方的二维码，来获取下方听力理解文章的音频录音。或者，请求他人帮你进行阅读。认真听写文章内容并且回答以下问题。

什么是二维码？ 二维码与条形码类似，是一种可应用手机的照相设备进行扫描的在线内容链接方式，使你不必在你的手机浏览器中输入繁琐的链接地址。

Questions 1 - 4 refer to the following passage.

Passage 1 - Caterpillars

Butterflies and moths have a three stage life cycle. Caterpillars are the first or laval stage. Caterpillars can be either herbivores, feeding mostly on plants, or carnivores, feeding on other insects. Caterpillars eat continuously. Once they are too big for their body, they shed or molt their skin.

Some caterpillars have symbiotic relationships with other insects. A symbiotic relationship is where different species work together in a way that is either harmful or helpful. Symbiotic relationships are critical to many species and ecosystems.

Some caterpillars and ants have a symbiotic or mutual relationship where both benefit. Ants give some protection, and caterpillars provide the ants with honeydew nectar.

Ants and caterpillars communicate by vibrations through the soil as well as grunting and squeaking. Humans are not able to hear these communications.

Scan for audio or Click

1. What do most larvae spend their time doing?

    a. Eating

    b. Sleeping

    c. Communicating with ants.

    d. None of the above

2. Are all caterpillars herbivores?

    a. Yes

    b. No, some eat insects

3. What benefit do larvae get from association with ants?

    a. They do not receive any benefit.

    b. Ants give them protection.

    c. Ants give them food.

    d. Ants give them honeydew secretions.

4. Do ants or larvae benefit most from association?

    a. Ants benefit most
    b. Larvae benefit most
    c. Both benefit about the same
    d. Neither benefits

Questions 5 - 7 refer to the following passage.

Passage 2 - Fire

Fire is a chemical reaction producing light, flames, heat and generally smoke. This reaction is an example of rapid oxidation.

Other types of oxidation, such as rust or digestion occur very slowly in comparison.

The visible part of the chemical reaction, the flame, is different colors depending on the material burning. The flame is incandescent particles of soot. With more oxygen, the fire reaction is hotter and burns more cleanly, producing less soot, and the flame turns blue. Many fires burn at 1000 degrees Celsius (1800 Fahrenheit).

Scan for audio or click
https://www.test-preparation.ca/audio/Fire-2.mp3

5. Are oxidation processes like rust the same as fire?

   a. Yes
   b. No

6. What causes flames to have different colors?

   a. The heat of the fire
   b. The material burning
   c. Impurities in the surrounding air
   d. None of the above

Questions 7 – 9 refer to the following passage.

Passage 3 - Gardens

Roman gardens were initially built to supply the household with vegetables and herbs. Later, the influence from Greek and Persian gardens changed Roman gardens to pleasure gardens in palaces and villas, as well as public parks meant for enjoyment and exercise. At this time Roman gardens had their famous statues and sculptures.

Later with the fall of the Roman Empire, gardening declined and during the Middle Ages, gardening was strictly for herbs used in various medicines, and for decorating churches.

Persian garden were surrounded by walls and meant to look like paradise. Traditional Islamic gardens are heavily influence by the desert, an important part of Persian culture. Therefore, water and shade are important elements. Gardens, in Islamic culture, are for meditation and rest. Sunlight is an important feature of Persian gardens and often the architecture, layout and textures highlight reflected sunlight. Persian gardens are built on an indoor/outdoor plan that often uses courtyards.

Scan for audio or click
https://www.test-preparation.ca/audio/Gardens-2.mp3

7. What is a characteristic feature of Roman gardens?

    a. Statues and Sculptures

    b. Flower beds

    c. Medicinal Herbs

    d. Courtyard gardens

8. When did gardening decline?

    a. Before the Fall of Rome.

    b. Gardening did not decline.

    c. Before the Middle Ages.

    d. After the Fall of Rome.

9. What kind of gardening was done during the Middle Ages?

    a. Gardening with hedges and vines

    b. Gardening with a wide variety of flowers

    c. Gardening for medicinal plants and decorating churches

    d. Gardening divided by watercourses

Questions 10 – 12 refer to the following passage.

Passage 4 - Insect Pests

A pest is an organism that is destructive to crops, humans, structures, or other animals. Insect pests make up about 1% of the insect family. Many insects such as bees and silkworms are beneficial.

Many blood-sucking insects carry diseases the pick up from infected hosts and pass on.

Some insects that were previously harmless, can become pests if they are introduced to a new area. In the new area often insects do not have natural predators.

Often insects carry diseases. The common housefly breeds on organic wastes and can carry diseases to food which is consumed by humans.

Pests can be controlled using insecticides and introducing natural predators. For example, farmers introduce predators such as ladybugs to their crops to control various insect pests.

Scan for audio or click
https://www.test-preparation.ca/audio/InsectPests-2.mp3

10. How do humans control insects?

    a. By training them
    b. Using insecticides and other techniques
    c. In many different ways
    d. Humans don't control insects

11. What are examples of beneficial insects?

    a. Cows and bats
    b. Bees and silkworms
    c. Caterpillars and ants
    d. None of the above

12. What percent of insects are pests?

    a. 5%
    b. 10%
    c. 1%
    d. 3%

Questions 13 - 15 refer to the following passage.

Insects

Insects were the first animals able to fly. Most, but not all insects have wings, and all have six legs. Their life-cycle varies but most hatch eggs. Insects undergo a transformation process, called metamorphosis, where the immature insects undergo two or three stages. Insects outgrow their bodies and shed, or molt their old body several times.

Adult insects walk, sometimes swim, or fly.

Most insects have a walking style called tripedal. In this walking style or gait, their six legs touch the ground in alternating triangles. This gait allows for very rapid movement. Insects are mostly solitary but some, such as ants or bees live in colonies. Even though insect colonies have hundreds of individuals, they function together as one organism.

Insects are found all over the world, in virtually every environment. A few even live in the ocean. Some insects feed on fruit and crops and are classified as pests, and controlled with pesticides and other means. Others perform complex ecological roles and some spread disease.

Insects communicate in a variety of ways. For example, some insects, like crickets, produce a sound, by rubbing their legs together. Some beetles communicate with light.

Scan for audio or click
https://www.test-preparation.ca/audio/Insects-2.mp3

13. Choose the correct sentence.

    a. No insects can swim.

    b. All insects are excellent swimmers.

    c. Some insects can swim.

    d. Most insects can swim.

14. Choose the correct sentence.

    a. All insects communicate with sound.
    b. No insects communicate with sound.
    c. Insects don't communicate
    d. Some insects communicate with sound.

15. Are insects solitary or social?

    a. Solitary
    b. Social
    c. Some are social and some are solitary
    d. None of the above

Questions 16 - 17 refer to the following passage.

Trees

Trees are an essential part of our natural ecosystem and provide shelter, fuel, medicine and much more. One of the principal benefits of trees is the photosynthesis process where carbon dioxide is absorbed, and oxygen released. Trees are also important in preventing erosion. Trees remove many types of pollutants in addition to carbon dioxide.

Trees have many practical applications. Wood is a fuel for heat as well as cooking for much of the world. Timber is used for construction, and pulp from wood is used to make paper.
Tree bark provides important medicines such as aspirin and quinine.

Scan for Audio or go to
https://www.test-preparation.ca/audio/Trees-2.mp3

16. What are two reasons trees are important in the natural landscape?

a. They prevent erosion and produce oxygen.

b. They produce fruit and are important elements in c. landscaping.

c. Trees are not important in the natural landscape.

d. Trees produce carbon dioxide and prevent erosion.

17. What do trees do to the atmosphere?

a. Trees produce carbon dioxide and reduce oxygen.

b. Trees produce oxygen and carbon dioxide.

c. Trees reduce oxygen and carbon dioxide.

d. Trees produce oxygen and reduce carbon dioxide.

Conversation 1 - Ordering at the Restaurant

Questions 18 - 20 refer to the following conversation.

Narrator: Carol, Tom, Sarah and Peter order dinner at Marina's Gourmet Restaurant. The waiter is at their table.

Waiter: Hello. What would you like to have, today?

Peter: I would like to have the fish. Please.

Tom: I would like to have the steak.

Carol: I would like the fish, please.
Sarah: I like chicken. Chicken, please.

Narrator: The waiter goes to get their dinners.

Carol: The dinners are expensive! I hope they are good.

Scan for Audio or go to
https://www.test-preparation.ca/audio/Resurant-1.mp3

18. What kind of restaurant are they at?

   a. Gourmet
   b. Hotel restaurant
   c. Fast food
   d. None of the above

19. What does Carol hope?

   a. She hopes the dinners are not expensive
   b. She hopes the dinners are good
   c. She hopes the fish is fresh
   d. She hopes the steak is cooked properly

20. How many people order pasta?

   a. They all have pasta
   b. Nobody orders pasta
   c. 2 people order pasta
   d. 3 people order pasta

Conversation 2 - At the Restaurant

Questions 21 - 22 refer to the following conversation.

Narrator: The waiter at Marina's Gourmet Restaurant brings the dinners for Carol, Tom, Sarah and Peter.

Waiter: Enjoy your dinners.

Sarah: Thank you, they look good.

Peter: I like this fish.

Tom: This steak is tasty!

Carol: This fish is good!

Tom: This restaurant is expensive but I like it.

Scan for Audio or go to
https://www.test-preparation.ca/audio/Resturant-2.mp3

21. Does everyone enjoy their dinner?

    a. Yes
    b. No

22. What does the waiter say when he brings their dinners?

    a. He doesn't say anything
    b. Enjoy your dinners
    c. Let me know if you need anything
    d. Your dinners look good

Conversation 3 - At Home

Questions 23 - 24 refer to the following conversation.

Narrator: You are at home. Your friend visits you.

You: Hello, please come in.

Your friend: Thanks.

You: Would you like some tea or coffee?

Your friend: I would like some tea.

You: I like tea, too.

Scan for Audio or go to
https://www.test-preparation.ca/audio/AtHome.mp3

23. Do all the friends like tea?

    a. Yes
    b. No

24. Where are they?

    a. At home
    b. At a restaurant
    c. Downtown
    d. At a hotel

Conversation 4 - Outside

Questions 25 refers to the following conversation.

Narrator: Sarah, Peter, Tom and Carol walk outside.

They talk about the dinner.

Peter: That is a good restaurant.

Tom: They have good music, too.

Sarah: I enjoy the music.

Tom: So do I!

Carol: The waiter is friendly, too.

Tom: It is expensive but I like it.

Scan for Audio or go to https://www.test-preparation.ca/audio/Outside.mp3

25. What are the friends talking about?

    a. The weather
    b. Work
    c. The weekend
    d. The restaurant

应答键

1. A
Caterpillars spend most of their time eating.

2. B
Some caterpillars are herbivores, others eat other insects (carnivores).

3. B
From the passage, the ants provide some degree of protection.

4. C
The association is mutual so they both benefit.

5. B
Fire is an oxidation process but is much faster than rust or digestion.

6. B
Depending on the materials burning, the flame is a different color.

7. A
Roman gardens are known for their statues and sculptures.

8. D
After the fall of Rome, gardening declined.

9. C
From the passage, "during the Middle Ages, gardening was strictly for herbs used in various medicines, and for decorating churches."

10. B
The techniques for controlling insects is taken from the last paragraph.

11. B
Bees and silkworms are examples of beneficial insects.

12. C
1% of the insect family are pests.

13. C
From the passage, "Adult insects walk, sometimes swim, or fly."

14. D
From the passage, "For example, some insects, like crickets, produce a sound, ..."

15. C
Insects are mostly solitary, but some, such as ants and bees, live in colonies.

16. A
Choice A is a re-wording of text from the passage.

17. D
This question is designed to confuse by presenting different options for the 2 chemicals, oxygen and carbon dioxide. One is produced and one is reduced.

18. A
They are at a gourmet restaurant.

19. B
Carol hopes the meals are good because they are expensive.

20. B
Nobody orders pasta.

21. A
Yes everyone enjoys their dinner.

22. B
The waiter says, "Enjoy your dinners" when he brings them.

23. A
Yes all of the friends like tea.

24. A
They are at home.

25. D
They are talking about the restaurant.

如何写作文

写作是一个复杂的过程，特别是当你在有时间限制的考试中。这里是三个简单的步骤，它们可以帮助你写出一个完整，符合逻辑的文章：

1. 头脑风暴帮你提供你文章的潜在主题内容以及整体思路。
2. 罗列你每一部分的内容大纲，以及容易理解的副标题。
3. 完成你的写作，要注意正确恰当的语法和句子结构。

头脑风暴

首先你应该花一点时间想想你文章的中心主题是什么。如果写作题目有给出问题，你必须要确定你的文章能够完整的回答问题。在题目要求中划出关键词可能会对你有帮助，或者利用蜘蛛网图来记下你的大体思路。

例题

阅读下面的信息并完成题目要求：

Joseph Conrad is a Polish author who lived in England for most of his life and wrote a prolific amount of English literature. Much of his work was completed during the height of the British Empire's colonial imperialism. Assignment: What impact has Joseph Conrad had on modern society? Present your point of view on the matter and support it with evidence. Your evidence may include reasoning, logic, examples from readings, your own experience, and observations.

约瑟夫 康拉德

> **背景？** 水手，探险，波兰移民，青年，诺斯托罗莫，黑暗之心
> **他的写作主题？** 象牙，银器交易，殖民主义，腐败，贪婪
> **思路？** 逐渐进入疯狂，邪恶的本质

提纲（或计划）

提纲或计划对于你完整有逻辑的组织你的思路是十分重要的。记录提纲的方法有很多；最简单的方法就是先罗列出以下四点内容：

1. 标题
2. 起始段
3. 文章主题
4. 总结

然后，你需要写下每一项标题下的主要思路和主题内容并使它们具有相应的逻辑性。这份提纲现在就是你文章的主要依据。

提示：即时没有要求必须写出一份写作的提纲和计划，你也应该将这些内容写在答题册或者试卷的背面并养成这个习惯。简单的划出一条线并写出"计划"或者"提纲"。这种方法可以向读者更好的展示你是如何完成写作规划和写作内容的。

写作文

你的起始段可以帮助读者来决定是否要继续阅读你文章后面的内容。起始段同时也介绍了你文章的主旨以及向读者提供文章的背景介绍。第一句话是非常关键的，你应当避免使用"I will be comparing…"这样的句子作为文章的起始句。

范文

Born as Józef Teodor Konrad Korzeniowski on December 3rd, 1857, Joseph Conrad led an adventurous life. As a Polish immigrant, Conrad never quite fit into England where he spent most of his adult life. As a younger man, Conrad made a living off sailing voyages. These swashbuckling experiences soon had him writing tales of the high seas such as one of his first works, Youth. While his early, adventurous work was of high quality, Conrad is best remembered for shedding light on the exploitative side of colonialism. Age and experience led him to start writing about (and challenging) the darker side of the imperial way of thinking. Conrad's work has forever soured words such as colonialism and imperialism.

在主体部分，或者你文章的正文中，你要确保文章的独特性和原创性。
避免陈词滥调的使用。

注意你的语气。
考虑你语言的使用。避免使用行业术语和俚语。尽量使用目的明确和具有形象化描述的写作方法。

你的写作内容要保持流畅；要体现出过渡，特别是段落之间。大声朗读出你段首的句子来确保它们的正确使用。
尽量在新的段落中使用新的概念或想法。

范文

Conrad's written fiction focused on themes such as greed and power. He portrayed these two concepts as purveyors of evil. Greed and power may take on different guises, but the end result would always be the same.

Perhaps his most famous piece, The Heart of Darkness, is about the descent of an English ivory trader, Mr. Kurtz, into madness. We are taken up a river resembling the Congo by a narrator, Marlow, who is sent to retrieve Mr. Kurtz. Marlow eventually finds that Kurtz has been diluted by power and greed, the two things that spurred on colonialism in Africa. Kurtz has 102 taken charge of a large tribe of natives (that he brutalizes) and has been hoarding ivory for himself. Much of Conrad's later work was cut from the same vein as The Heart of Darkness. His crowning achievement is considered Nostromo where he takes an idealistic hero and corrupts him with colonial greed. Only this time the greed is for silver, not ivory.

Conrad's work resonates with readers partly because it was semi-autobiographical. Where his experience sailing the high seas helped bring his adventure stories to light, likewise did his experience witnessing atrocities in Africa reverberate through his writing.

文章的总阶段是你最后能抓住的机会，通过这部分内容来感染你的读者并向他们传达你整篇文章的逻辑思路。最好能够使你结尾段和起始段的内容进行首尾呼应，或者提供一些总结性的陈述。如果你不能完整的进行收尾，千万不要慌乱。大多数部分的题目都是有开放性答案的。

你的结尾段应当始终和文章其他的内容相呼应，结尾的内容不应该添加任何新的想法和思路。同样重要的是，一个失败的结尾段可能会大大缩减一篇好文章的效果。

范文

In sum, Joseph Conrad's life experiences and masterful writing left a lasting impact on the image of progress and what it meant to "move forward." He brought to light the cost in human lives that was required for Europe to continue mining natural resources from foreign lands. Joseph Conrad had a permanent impact on imperial culture, and colonial brutality has been on the decline ever since his work was published.

写作质量

即使是一篇优秀的文章，过多的语法和标点错误也可能使其功亏一篑。你应当按照写作要求中的每一项要求来完成写作，例如字数要求。要确保你的字迹是清楚可辨的。尽量在交卷之前留出一些时间来从头到尾的阅读你的文章以确保万无一失。

提示：如果条件允许，每隔一行进行写作。如果你在书写时出现任何错误，可以将错误的地方划掉并将正确的内容写在空白行中。

以下是一些可以使你的文章增光添彩的技巧：
好的作文一般都会有一个明确的中心思想。

没有固定的写作结构，但是你可以使用副标题来提升阅读性。

避免使用具有特殊敏感性或者争论性的话题。如果你一定要写一些具有争论性的话题，那么要确保你的内容中包含争论双方的内容。
重要的不是你的文章与主题本身的相关性有多大；而是通过主题你在文章中发挥的内容。

你的文章中可以包含你通过平时的阅读，经历，学习或者观察的例子。

花些时间练习写作并且在考试前多阅读范文。

示例 让我们来看另一个范文，它同样应用了之前所提到的写出好文章的三个必要步骤：

1. 头脑风暴
2. 列出提纲
3. 完成写作

通过这篇文章，我们可以更清楚的理解三个必要步骤的使用方法。

头脑风暴示例

> *Think about the information that follows and the assignment below.*
>
> *People often quote the last two lines of Robert Frost's "The Road not Taken" as being metaphorical for success. The line's read "I took the one less travelled by, / And that has made all the difference" (19, 20).*
>
> *Assignment: Analyze and interpret this poem. Consider the poem's place in Modernist culture and Robert Frost's personal experiences. Read in between the lines and identify the more complex aspects/themes of this poem. Outline and complete an essay that challenges the point of view presented above, that the poem is synonymous with success. Provide evidence backed up by logic, experience, research, and/ or examples from the poem.*

上方的题目要求以及关键词已经被标记出来。可以确定的是这篇文章不是在问一个问题，而是要求对主题内容进行讨论。

现在需要花点时间来记录一些关于题目的想法。在头脑风暴这一步，先不需要太在意语法问题，只需要把你想到的信息记录下来就可以：

"The Road Not Taken" by Robert Frost

背景？现代主义诗歌艺术
主题？人生的抉择，悔恨，命运，以及未知的将来
思路？分岔路是象征的手法，最后的叹息表示了悔恨，人生道路上有很多的崎岖和转折，你当下做的一个简单决定可能会使你的人生发生翻天覆地的变化。

提纲（或计划）
列出提纲或计划是写作中第二个非常关键的步骤，你应当花几分钟认真的完成这一步。这个计划和你最后的文章是同等重要的。你也可以在提纲中标记出你完成每一部分所需要的时间。确保为每部分文章的内容写出标题，并且在标题下方写下你想要探讨的问题/主题。

示例

1. Title
2. Essay introduction
Identify and discuss the underlying theme/s in Robert Frost's "The Road Not Taken"
What was Frost's background and its applicability to understanding this poem?
3. Essay body
Quick summary of the poem
Discuss key themes and other concepts
Discuss how these things relate to Modernism
4. Essay conclusion
Rephrase the themes of Robert Frost's poem and their place in modernist doctrine

这份提纲现在就是你完成这篇文章的依据。

完成写作

起始段是十分重要的，因为它的作用是要向读者介绍文章

的大体内容，使读者可以有兴趣阅读后面的内容。一个好的起始段会向读者介绍相关的重要信息，使他们在阅读文章后面内容的时候能有更好的理解。

范文

> 确定并讨论在Robert Frost的"The Road Not Taken"一文中的划线主题。

> *Robert Frost wrote during the artistic movement after World War I known as Modernism. One purpose of modernism was to remake things in a new light, to analyze and change symptoms of societies that had plunged the European world into a grisly war. Frost's poem, "The Road Not Taken," carries with it a burden of regret that was a staple of Modernist art.*

这个起始段一开始就介绍了Robert Frost所处的时期以及他的现实生活对他"The Road Not Take"这首诗的影响。这段内容中包含了强有力的语言，以此来鼓励读者继续阅读文章后面的内容，并且也为理解整篇文章的内容打下了坚实的基础。

主体部分或者你文章的正文内容也是十分重要的:

范文

> *"The Road Not Taken" was almost assuredly influenced by Robert Frost's personal life. He was very familiar with facing difficult decisions. Frost had to make the decision to send both his sister and daughter to mental institutions. His son Carol committed suicide at the age of 38. The list of loss Frost experienced in his life goes on, but it suffices to say he was familiar with questioning the past.*

With no other hints of the narrator's identity, it is best to assume that he is a man similar to Frost himself. The poem itself is about a nameless narrator reflecting on when he travelled through the autumn woods one day. He had come across a split in the road and expresses regret that he could not travel both. Each road is described as looking similar and as having equal wear but it is also mentioned one was grassier. The roads were unknown to the narrator, and also shared equal possibilities in how well they may or may not be around their bends. He tells his listener with a sigh that he had made his decision and had taken "the road less travelled by" (19). Even though he had little idea which road would be better in the long run, the one he chose proved difficult.

This poem is a collection of all the insecurities and possibilities that come with even the simplest decisions. We experience the sorrow expressed by the narrator in the opening lines with every decision we make. For all the choices you make in life, there is a counterweight of choices you have not made. In a way, we are all missing half of our lives' possibilities. This realization causes a mixture of regret and nostalgia, but also stokes in us the keen awareness these missed opportunities are inevitable and regretting them is a waste of energy. We often find ourselves stuck, as the narrator is, between questioning the decisions we've made and knowing that this natural process isn't exactly productive.

Unsolvable regret and nostalgia are things that the Modernists fought with on a regular basis. They often experimented *in taking happenings of the past and reinventing them to fit a new future.*

文章主体内容一开始对Robert Frost的生平进行了介绍，以及他的人生经历，与他的诗歌"The Road Not Taken"中难以抉择这个主题的相关性。

在非常恰当的位置另起一段，上一段谈及了Robert Frost的生平，过渡句的使用将读者带回书的开头（对上一段文字的内容进行收尾）。这样可以帮助读者将注意力集中到下一个讨论点。

这篇文章的语气是正式的，主要是因为主题的严肃性 – 在全世界，怀念和悔恨都在人们的生活中占领了及其重要的位置。

关于结尾部分的内容，其中会有一个关于主要讨论内容的总结。理想的效果是你能够利用你的文章来感染读者，更重要的是，你要确定总结段中包含了你之前涉及的所有内容，并且对于你讨论过的关键点，给出恰当的总结性陈述。

范文

In conclusion, Robert Frost's poem "The Road Not Taken" deals with themes of fate, regret, sorrow, and the many possibilities our decisions hold. Consider how easy it would be to upturn your life today if you made a few decisions you normally wouldn't. Frost's poem forces us to consider the twists and turns our lives take. Perhaps with a sigh, we could all think about the choices that for us have made all the difference.

这个总结段中的内容与文章其他部分在风格上完全一致。当中没有介绍新的想法，并且与题目中的主要论点具有相关性。

最后，在提交试卷之前要把你的文章通读一遍。只需要花几分钟来阅读并找出错误。记住在写作的过程中每隔一行来书写，这样可以给你之后的修改留出空间。你也可以在每段之间留出空档，如果你想添加一到两句话时可以有足够的位置。

写作中的常见错误 – 示例 1

Whether the topic is love or action, reality television shows damage society. Viewers witness the personal struggles of strangers and they experience an outpouring of emotions in the name of entertainment. This can be dangerous on many levels. Viewers become numb to real emotions and values. <u>Run the risk of not interpreting a dangerous situation correctly.</u> 1 The reality show participant is also at risk because they are <u>completely exposed</u>. 2 The damage to both viewers and participants leads to the destruction of our healthy societal values.

<u>Romance reality shows are dangerous to the participants and contribute to the emotional problems witnessed in society today as we set up a system built on equality and respect, shows like "The Bachelor" tear it down.</u> 3 In front of millions of viewers every week, young women compete for a man. <u>Twenty-five women claim to be in love with a man they just met. The man is reduced to an object they compete for. There are tears, fights, and manipulation aimed at winning the prize.</u> 4 Imagine a young woman's reality when she returns home and faces the scrutiny of viewers who watched her unravel on television every Monday night. These women objectify themselves and <u>have learned</u> 5 that relationships are a combination of hysteria and competition. This does not give hope to a society based on family values and equality.

6 While incorporating the same manipulations and breakdown of relationships offered on "The Bachelor," shows like "Survivor" add another level of danger. Not only are they building a society based on lying to each other, they are competing in physical challenges that become dangerous. In the name of entertainment, these challenges become increasingly physical and are usually held in a hostile environment. The viewer's ability to determine the safety of an activity is <u>messed up.</u> 7 To entertain and preserve their pride, participants continue in competitions regardless of the danger level. <u>For example,</u> 8 participants on "Survivor" have sustained serious injuries in the form of heart attack and burns. Societal rules are based on the safety of its citizens, not on hurting yourself for entertainment.

Reality shows of all kinds are dangerous to participants. They damage society. 9

1. 改正不完整句子结构。Who/what runs the risk? 需要给这个句子添加一个主语或者把它和前面的句子进行整合。可以修改为:"Viewers become numb to real emotions and run the risk of not interpreting a dangerous situation correctly."

2. 改正多余的词语表达。可以修改为:"The reality show participant is also at risk because they are exposed."

3. 改正连缀句。考虑一下如何将句子进行分割。可以修改为:"Romance reality shows are dangerous to participants and contribute to the emotional problems of society today. As we support a system built on equality and respect, shows like "The Bachelor" tear it down."

4. 调整句子结构和长度。可以修改为:"Twenty-five women claim to be in love with a man who is reduced to being the object of competition. There are tears, fights, and manipulation aimed at winning the prize."

5. 使用主动语态。可以修改为: "These women objectify themselves and learned that relationships are a combination of hysteria and competition."

6. 使用过渡句将两个段落进行连接。可以修改为: "Action oriented reality shows are equally as dangerous to the participants."

7. 避免使用非正式语言/俚语。可以修改为: "The viewer's ability to determine the safety of an activity is compromised."

8. 不要对文章内容进行强调。避免使用 "for example" 和 "in conclusion" 这样的词组。可以修改为: "Participants on "Survivor" have sustained serious injuries as heart attack and burns."

9. 给你自己留出时间来写出一个强有力的总结段！例如: 为最后的总结内容预留出3-5分钟。

写作中的常见错误 – 示例 2

Questioning authority makes society stronger. <u>In every aspect our society, there is an authoritative person or group making rules. There is also the group underneath them who are meant to follow.</u> 1 This is true of our country's public schools as well as our federal government. The right to question authority at both of these levels is guaranteed by the United States Declaration of Independence. <u>People are given the ability to question so that authority figures are kept in check</u> 2 and will be forced to listen to the opinions of other people. Questioning authority leads to positive changes in society and preserves what is already working well.

If students never question the authority of a principal's decisions, the best interest of the student body is lost. <u>Good things </u>3 may not remain in place for the students and no amendment to the rules are sought. Change requires that authority be questioned. An example of this is Silver Head Middle School in Davie, Florida. Last year, the principal felt strongly about enforcing the school's uniform policy. <u>Some students were not bothered by this</u>. 4 Many students felt the policy disregarded their civil rights. A petition voicing student dissatisfaction was signed and presented to the principal. He met with a student representative to discuss the petition. Compromise was reached as a monthly "casual day." The students were able to promote change and peace by questioning authority.

Even at the level of federal government, our country's ultimate authority, the ability to question is the key to the harmony keeping society strong. <u>Most government officials are elected by the public so they have the right to question their authority</u>. 5 If there's a mandate, law, or statement that citizens aren't 6 happy with, they have recourse. Campaigning for or against a political platform and participating in the electoral process give a voice to every opinion. I think elections are <u>very important</u>. 7 Without this questioning and examination of society's laws, the government will represent only the voice of the authority figure. The success of our society is based on the questioning of authority. 8
Society is strengthened by those who question authority. Dialogue is created between people with different visions and change becomes possible. At both the level of public school and of federal

government, the positive effects of questioning authority can be witnessed. Whether questioning the decisions of a single principal or the motives of the federal government, it is the willingness of people to question and create change that allows society to grow. <u>A strong society is inspired by many voices, all at different levels.</u> 9 These voices keep society strong.

1. 言简意赅。 将句子进行整合并删除多余的单词。可以修改为:"In every aspect of society, there is an authority making rules and a group of people meant to follow them."

2. 避免使用俚语。 替换 "kept in check"。可以修改为:"People are given the ability to question so that authority figures are held accountable and will be forced to listen to the opinions of other people."

2-2. 删除不必要的词。 可以修改为:"People are given the ability to question so that authority figures are held accountable and will listen to other opinions."

3. 使用准确的语言进行描述。 什么是 "good things"？可以修改为:"Interesting activities may not remain in place for the students and no amendment to the rules are sought."

使用正确的主谓一致关系。 要准确的找出你句子中正确的主语。可以修改为:"Interesting activities may not remain in place for the students and no amendment to the rules is sought."

4. 不要随意添加那些不能给你的内容增光添彩的信息。 删除 "Some students weren't bothered by this."

5. 检查你句子的平行结构。 是谁有权利来质疑谁的权利？可以修改为:"Having voted them in, the people have the authority to question public officials."

6. 在学术性文章中不要使用缩写。 可以修改为："If there is a mandate, law, or statement that citizens are not happy with, they have recourse."

7. 在说服类文章中不要使用代词"I"。 把"I think elections are very important." 这句话删除。

8. 使用特殊的例子来印证你的观点。例如：深入的讨论一个特殊的选举内容。

9. 删除繁冗的句子。 删除"A strong society is inspired by many voices, all at different levels."

言简意赅

简明扼要的写作方式是具有直接性和有效描述性的。读者可以轻松的跟随作者的思路。如果你的文章内容简洁明了，一个由四个段落组成的文章是完全能够到达标准考试要求的。对于观点的描述不在于数量多少，而是在于对每个观点描述的质量。

但这并不是说文章的字数越少越好。要知道你在文章中所使用的每一个词都是十分重要的。不必要的或者是重复的信息可能会稀释或者减弱你文章的质量。Concise这个词的意思来源于拉丁语，意思是"切碎"。如果是不必要的信息，就不要使用考试中宝贵的时间写出来。

对内容进行重复阐述是一个增长句子或者段落长度最简单的方法，但是在限时的作文中，这一方法会对你的文章产生反作用。虽然有很多人使用重复的词组或者措辞来给自己加分，但是不能给文章增光添彩的词是没有保留价值的。内容过于重复会对读者造成迷惑，并且在你快速书写的情况下很容易跑题。要注意，有很多的繁冗词组都来自于我们的日常生活，需要你将它们剔除出去。

例如，"bouquet of flowers"就是一个重复词组，因为只有"bouquet"是必须的。它的定义中包含了flowers的意思。

特别要注意你在强调某一观点时所使用的词，例如"completely"，"totally"，和"very"。

First of all, I'd like to thank my family.
修改为：First, I'd like to thank my family. 首先，我要感谢我的家人。

The school *introduced a new rule*.。
修改为：The school introduced a rule. **学校发布了新的校规。**

I am *completely full*.
修改为：I am full. 我吃的太饱了。

Your glass is *totally empty*!
修改为：Your glass is empty! 你的杯子是空的！

Her artwork is *very unique*.
修改为：Her artwork is unique. 她的艺术作品是独一无二的。

其他一些包括删减内容和时间的方法，也例如删除那些对于你的文章没有作用或者实际意义的词组。例如"in my opinion"，"as a matter of fact"，以及"due to the fact that"这些都是浪费时间和写作空间的。除此之外，要把被动语态转化为主动语态。

In my opinion, the paper is well written.
修改为：The paper is well written. 这篇文章写的很不错。

The book *was written* by the best students.
修改为：The best students wrote the book. 这是最出色的学生写的书。

The teacher *is listening* to the students.
修改为：The teacher listens to the students. 老师听取了学生所说的话。

这种方法是主题内容得到了充分的解释，缩短并精简了句子的内容。当你在写作时间有限的情况下，简明扼要的语言会给你提供极大的帮助。

这个方法不仅仅适用于单词和词组，毫无意义的句子也应当从文章中删除。将通用名词换成特定名词是一种比较有效的方法。

She screamed as the thing came closer. It was a sharp-toothed dog.
修改为：She screamed as the sharp-toothed dog came closer. 当尖牙狗靠近她时，她开始大叫。

通过对句子的简化，段落的内容也通过句子结构的整合与变化得到了有效的提升。在校对的时候，问问自己哪些思路应当进行连接，而哪些需要被分离。每当你写完一段都要进行一下快速阅读并且在适当的位置进行段落分割。

留出三到四分钟时间来进行最后的校对工作。在通读文章时，在每一个句号的位置做一个标记。这个方法可以使你"听"到读者在阅读文章时的感受，而不是你想传达给他们的内容。这样可以帮助你找到需要删减或组合的词组和句子。这也是作文考试中的一项评分标准。

避免词句的重复使用

在英语中，重复和繁冗是指使用两个或两个以上的词来表达相同的意思，使其中的一个或多个内容成为多余的内容。在英语口语中，经常会在对话中使用重复的表达或词组，但这是一种常见的情况，然而在书面英语中，重复是一个严肃的问题并且不容忽视。以下是一些词汇重复的例子。

1. Suddenly exploded.
An explosion指的就是突如其来的或者立刻发生的事件，已经充分表示出sudden的意思。不需要在exploded前面使用"suddenly"修饰。

2. Final outcome.
An outcome指的是结果。An outcome本身就有final的意思，所以没有必要再用final修饰outcome。

3. Advance notice/planning/reservations/warning.
A warning, notice, reservation or plan都是在事件发生前需要做的准备工作。一旦读者看到这类词的使用，他们就会知道这些已经在事件发生前完成了。所以这些词不需要再与advance一同使用。

4. First began, new beginning.
Beginning表示事情的起始或者第一次，所以使用"new"是不必要的。

5. Add an additional.
"add"这个词表示的是提供其他内容的意思，因此"additional"这个词的使用是不必要的。

6. For a period/number of days.
"days"这个词本身已经是复数，并且清楚的表明了大于一天的意思。因此使用"a number of"或者"a period of"来修饰days有些累赘。number of days 或者 of the specific number of days的说法是不正确的, 正确的说法是"many days"。

7. Foreign imports.
Imports 这个词本身就包含国外的意思，因为进口是指物品从另一国家进入，所以用"foreign"这个词修饰有些多余。

8. Forever and ever.
Forever 表示永久永恒的意思，因此不需要在其后面使用"ever"来与forever这个词重复。

9. Came at a time when.
"At a time" 在这个词组中是不必要的，因为"when"已经表明了对动作coming时间上的修饰。

10. Free gift.
如果是花钱买的东西就不能算是gift。通常来说，gift都是免费的，所以用free修饰这个词有些重复。

11. Collaborate/join/meet/merge together.
merge, join, meet and collaborate 这几个词本身就是建议人或者事物合并到一起。所以没有必要再用together这个词进行修饰，例如merge together 或者 join together。正确的表达应该是删除together，只使用join或者merge。

12. Invited guests.
Guests 是被邀请来参加活动的人。如果被邀请的人才能称之为guests，那么就没有必要再用invited来修饰guests。

13. Major breakthrough.
breakthrough 本身是具有重要含义的。只有当具有重大进展和突破的时候才能称之为breakthrough。当你使用"breakthrough"这个词时，已经表明了过程的重要性，所以再使用"major"就会过于重复。

14. Absolutely certain or sure/essential/guaranteed.
当将某些人或事用sure或者certain进行修饰时，表明了他们是毫无疑问的态度。除了certain或者sure以外再使用"absolutely"是不必要的。essential 或者 guaranteed **也是表示事物的绝对性，所以也没有必要在后面使用**absolutely进行修饰。

15. Ask a question.
Ask表示提问的意思。所以在其后面使用"question"是多余的。

16. Basic fundamentals/essentials.
Basic的使用是多余的。Essentials和fundamental都是表示事物基本的性质。

17. [Number] a.m. in the morning/p.m. in the evening.
当你写出 8 a.m. 时，读者自然就知道你想表达的是上午8点整。因此没有必要说 8 a.m. in the morning。可以简化成 8 a.m. 或者 8 p.m.。

18. Definite decision.
即使以后仍可以修改，decision也是一个已经确定的事情。决定可以是一个被选择确认的行为。所以不需要用definite这个词再来修饰decision。

19. Past history/record.
record 或者 history 在定义上指的是过去发生的活动或事件。因此使用past修饰history 或者 record是没有必要的。

20. Consensus of opinion.
Consensus 指的是对某一事件或事物产生共识，未必指的是opinion。虽然看起来好像使用"consensus of opinion"更恰当，但是更建议删除"opinion"。

21. Enter in.
Enter 的意思是进入里面，因为没有人会进入外面。因此没有必要再说明in，直接说"enter"就可以。

22. Plan ahead.
你不可以为已经过去的事情做计划。Planning只能是为将来的事情打算。当你使用"plan"这个词的时候，已经表明了将来的意思。

23. Possibly might.
might 和 possibly 分别是用来形容不可能性的词，所以每次只能用一个。

24. Direct confrontation.
confrontation 指的是正面的冲突，所以不需要用"direct"进行修饰。

25. Postpone until later.
事件postponed指的是推迟或者改到后面的另一时间，因此不需要再用"later"来修饰。

26. False pretense.
Pretense 这个词只能用于欺骗行为，所以 "false" pretense 这个表达是多余的。

27. Protest against.
Protest 有对抗的含义在里面；因此不需要再在后面使用 against。

28. End result.
最后产生的才能事result。当读者看到"result"这个词的时候，已经知道事情已经发展到最后的阶段。

29. Estimated at about/roughly.
Estimates指的是对不能准确发生的事件的一个预估表达，因此不需要再用 "roughly" 或者 "about" 修饰。

30. Repeat again.
Repeat 指的是重复做某一件事，因此不需要用"again" 修饰。

31. Difficult dilemma.
dilemma 是指进退两难的状态，因此不需要再用"difficult"进行修饰。

32. Revert back.
Revert 是指返回到前面或者之前的状态。有的时候也指返回到过去的某个状态。因此不需要加 back。

33. (During the) course (of).
During 指的是"在...时候或期间"，不需要使用 "course" 来修饰。

34. Same identical.
Same 和 identical 指的是相同的意思，不应同时使用。

35. Completely filled/finished/opposite.
Completely 指的是完全的意思。然而，finished 和 filled 这两个词已经表明事物在某一程度上完全的状态。因此 finished 和 filled 不需要再用"completely"修饰。

36. Since the time when.
在这个词组表示中，"the time when"是不必要的因为"since"已经表示了过去的某一时间点。

37. Close proximity/scrutiny.
Proximity 指的是在距离上接近的意思。Scrutiny 指的是在学习上很仔细。不论是表明距离上接近的proximity，还是表明学习上仔细的scrutiny，两个词都有close的意思。因此没有必要把这些词放在一起使用。

38. Spell out in detail.
"Spell out" 意思是提供细节，所以不需要再在后面添加"in detail"。

39. Written down.
written 和 to be taken down是完全一样的意思。所以written应该单独使用。.

40. (Filled to) capacity.
任何事物 filled 指的是已经达到饱和，因此不需要再用capacity进行修饰。

41. Unintended mistake.
mistake 是指事物在非故意的情况下发生的错误。因此，缺少 intention 是显而易见的，不需要再用"unintended" 进行修饰。

42. Still remains.
"Remains" 表示事物持续在同一状态下，所以使用"still"有些多余。

43. Actual experience/fact.
事件在发生后称之为 experience 。如果没有发生就不能称作 experience。而 fact 只有在确认或确定的情况下才能定义为 fact。因此 experience 和 fact 这两个词都不需要用"actual"来修饰。

44. Therapeutic treatment.
Therapeutic 指的是疾病的治疗或康复。通常来说所有的 medical treatment 都属于therapeutic 因为它的目的是治疗或康复。因此当说到 medical treatment 的时候，没有必要再使用 therapeutic 来进行修饰。

45. At the present time.
"At present"这个词组指的是现在的时间或者"此时此刻"。"at the present time"是一种啰嗦的用法。最好直接使用"at present"。

46. Unexpected surprise.
surprise 是指非预期发生的情况。当看到或听到 surprised 这个词的时候会直接表达非预期的意思。因此不需要再用 unexpected 来修饰。

47. As for example.
"As"指的是 example 的使用，因此这个说法有点累赘。

48. Usual custom.
A custom 指的是某一事物被反复或日常的观察或完成。因此把"usual"和custom放在一起使用是不恰当的。

49. Added bonus.
Bonus 本身指的就是除了事物本身，多余出来的东西。因此使用"added"修饰bonus是不必要的。

50. Few in number.
Few表示事物数量上的少。因此不需要再用number修饰few。

如何应对口语考试

关于口语考试

对于大多数学生来说,尽管你觉得在备考方面,口试和笔试是类似的,但参加笔试和口语考试的经历是有很大区别的。

口语考试要求你向考官展示多项能力,其中包括:

1. 口语能力
2. 演讲能力
3. 交流能力

口试分为正式和非正式两种类型。正式的口语考试一般有先前规定好的题目,这一类型通常属于"竞争"类测试。非正式口语的限制要求比较少,并且你有机会来详尽阐释你的答案。

你的考官会根据你之前问题的作答内容来进行提问,考官希望你能够展示出例如问题解决能力等其他答题能力。

1. 口语考试中的问题一般为开放性问题,所以考生需要给出可供参考评估的答案,而不是简单的六个或七个单词。
2. 有些时候口语考试也会考察你了解多少相关领域的知识。

准备口语考试

准备口语考试有两个主要步骤。分别是调整和练习。

调整

和笔试一样,你会了解口语考试中会有哪些题目,因此对作答内容进行调整和修改是十分重要的。

列出你需要调整和修改的所有内容,并且多花一些时间来调整和修改你相对较弱的题目上。根据你所剩的备考时间进行合理安排,试着做出一个涵盖所有题目的学习计划。

除了调整和修改每一个答题内容,试着想想每个题目之间的联系,例如,X问题可行是由于Y问题中包含几个恰当回答X问题的内容。

有很多方法适用于修改和调整备考内容,其中包括:

使用目录卡并写下重点

1. 把要点写在便签上,并贴于房子的各处
2. 把笔记用录音记录下来并且进行回放
3. 向家人和朋友寻求意见和建议

对于每个人来说,修改和调整的方法都不是唯一的;你应当考虑在过去的口语和笔试中真正对你有帮助的方法。

1. 不要等到最后一分钟再调整和修改你的考试内容。
2. 提前思考你的主题中可能会被问道的问题。
3. 花一些时间来做练习题。
4. 请一位朋友来帮你做模拟练习(这样你可以基本了解你将会被问到的问题)。

练习

和调整一样,对于口语考试来说,练习也是很重要的。你会发现照镜子练习是十分有效的;通过这个方法你会找

到平时你和别人交谈时的习惯，例如拨弄头发或者坐立不安。

如果可以，你可以找机会来给自己做一段录音，这样你可以听一听自己的声音是什么样子的。

1. 当着其他人的面来做一些口语的题目练习。
2. 练习大声的讲话，确保所有人都能听到。
3. 练习减慢语速，你可能会发现你在口语考试中的语速过快，因为紧张会使人加快讲话的速度。
4. 练习用完整的句子进行表达。

如果英语是你的第二语言，尽可能多的和你身边所有英语是母语的人交谈。你也可以通过看英文电视，电影和听英文广播来学习和练习。

口语考试

考试前：

一定要提前到达考场，提前确认你的考试时间，日期和地点。

1. 关闭你的手机。
2. 思维灵活一些，很多人会把口语考试看成一次工作面试，所以和工作面试一样，第一印象永远是最重要的。
3. 考试前花几分钟来放松自己是十分有效的。试着做一次深呼吸，并重复这个动作10次。这个动作能帮助你平静下来。
4. 如果在考试中你会使用电脑或者投影仪等设备，提前确认它们都能正常工作。

考试期间：

1. 保持自信和微笑。

2. 尽量与考官保持眼神交流。

3. 保持正确的坐姿。

在回答问题之前深呼吸，做一个简短的停顿是会对你非常有帮助的。

1. 认真听考官说的内容。
2. 如果你不能完全理解问题的内容，可以请考官在重复一遍。
3. 避免天花乱坠的回答；如果你不知道答案可以告知考官。
4. 如果你觉得自己特别紧张，你可以向考官申请喝杯水，进行一个简短的暂停。
5. 在考试结束后要记得感谢考官。

如何备战考试

大多数学生在准备考试之前都是迟迟不肯动手的，特别是即将参加的考试是对他们未来有极大影响的时候，希望这样做可以减少考试给他们带来的痛苦。不敢面对考试是很多学生都会有的反应，然而不幸的是，由于缺乏准备，他们的结果都是惨痛的。

准备考试是需要策略的。同时也需要专心致志和持之以恒的态度。对任何一个对未来人生有规划的人来说，备战考试都是一次好的训练。除了需要几个有效策略以外，成功的学生还需要一个明确的目标以及如何完成目标的方法。把这些真实有效的方法实践成功就可以让你轻松备战。

学习方法。

自己负责考试备战。

我们经常会把自己的学习依赖于其他人身上，这是一个非常严重的错误。有学习伙伴很好，但是只有在彼此可以互帮互助的前提下才可以。即使你的学习伙伴不能帮到你，准备考试也是你自己的责任。千万不要让任何人打乱你的学习目标。

合理有效分配学习时间。

你什么时候的学习状态最好，清晨还是晚上？你是不是在零碎时间能够有效的吸收和保留信息呢，还是你需要长段的时间来完成？在你学习最高效的时候找到最佳学习时间是十分重要的。试着集中完成其他活动，这样可以留给你长段的学习时间。

找一个无人打扰的地方学习。

不要因为想在旧的地点学习而降低学习质量。尽可能找一个没有干扰的地方，例如图书馆，公园甚至是洗衣房。好的光线十分重要，并且你需要舒适的座位和一张能放下你学习材料的足够大的桌子。可能卧室不是一个适合学习的地方。地上的衣服，你打算读的书，电话或其他物品都有可能成为你的干扰。另外，在学习过程中，床看起来会是一个十分舒适的地方。不论你学习什么内容，不要在床上学习，因为你有可能会睡觉偷懒！上床睡觉是学习期间一定要避免的。

复习卡片是个例外。迄今为止，坐下安安静静的学习是最为有效的学习方法。然而，复习卡片是你可以随身携带并且可以随时随地学习的用品，例如你排队的时候或者等公交车的时候。虽然这种学习方法不能称之为有效，但是确是一件为你的复习提供帮助且值得你去做的事情。
确定你的学习材料。

整理你的书籍，笔记，电脑和其他有助于你复习的考试相关材料。复习之前确认你已经准备好所有材料，不会浪费学习时间。记得带纸，笔，橡皮，便签，水和零食。随身带着手机以便你在需要的时候查询重要信息。但是保持手机关机，使其他人不会打扰到你。

以乐观的态度面对考试。
在考试前的准备期间，保持一个良好的状态说 "我一定会通过的" 是十分重要的。并且挥舞着旗帜战胜考试吧！这是成功学习中的关键之一。对自我能力的坚信不疑可以使你无所不能。

学习方法

学习材料简单明了，方便获取。
对学习材料的整合不会让你的学习区域杂乱无章。如果你有电脑并且有网络连接，那么你就不需要字典或者词典，因为这些内容可以在网络上轻松获得。阅读你的笔记并且对内容进行整合。准备好所有需要的材料，但是不要让重复的复习内容对你造成压力。

复习课堂笔记。

通过经常的复习课堂笔记和作业来保持对知识的熟悉。重新记笔记是一个非常好的学习技巧，因为可以帮助你锁定重要信息。要特别注意任何老师留的评论。如果课堂上有使用任何类型的学习指导，好好利用这些材料！他们会是你学习和复习过程中非常有价值的工具。

预估你的学习时间。

如果你担心没有足够的时间准备考试的话，建议你建立一个学习时间表，使你不至于在某一部分停滞不前而没有时间来复习其他内容。记住要安排休息时间，利用这些时间来进行一些小运动或者减压活动。

通过自我测试来发现弱点。

通过网络找一些可用的测试和评估，例如特定科目的特定练习。一旦你发现了自己不足的地方，你可以集中练习这部分内容，并且对考试其他部分的内容进行巩固和提高。

精神准备 – 如何为考试做好心里准备

因为考试会极大程度的影响你最后的成绩或者决定你是否能被录取，因此可以理解，参加时头脑一片空白。你可以通过自我精神准备来避免焦虑。战胜焦虑的一个简单办法是通过几个简单的小技巧来做精神准备。

不要拖延。

从拿到复习材料那天开始考试复习，并且反复学习直到考试当天。拖到最后一分钟和填鸭式的方法会增加你的焦虑感。这样会导致你进行消极的自我对话，最后导致消极的自我预言。你自己说的 "I can't learn this. I am going to fail" 会得到印证。

积极的自我对话。

积极的自我对话可以压过消极的自我对话，并且增加你的自信。当你开始为考试感觉不知所措或者焦虑的时候，提醒自己说已经复习了足够多的材料，你已经熟知所有材料并且一定会通过考试。只用积极的词汇。不论积极还是消极自我对话都只不过是你的想象，所以为什么不对自己说好听的话呢？

不要用自己和他人比较。

不要用自己和其他学生做比较，或者拿你的表现和其他人的比较。相反的，你需要集中注意力找出你的强项和弱项，并相应的对其巩固和加强。不论其他人如何表现，你的表现才是决定你考试成绩的唯一条件。用你自己和其他人做比较只会增加你考试前的焦虑感和负面的自我对话。
想象力。

对你考试时的样子进行一个设想。你应答自如并且感觉很放松。想象你在考试中发挥的很好，并且对学习材料没有任何问题。想象力可以帮助你提升你的自信，以及减少你在考试前有可能会有的焦虑感。不要把这个过程看作是一个考试，而把它看作一个展示你学习成果的机会！
避免负面情绪。

焦虑会像病毒一样蔓延 – 一旦这种情绪开始就会一发不可收拾。因此需要在它成为问题之前就阻止它。即使你自己是放松和自信的状态，你身边同学焦虑和担心的情绪也会使你开始感到焦虑。考试之前，千万不要被其他同学的恐惧感所影响。考试之前有焦虑的担忧感是正常的，且每个学生体验到这种感受的时间点是相同的。但是重要的是你不能让这种负面情绪对你的发挥造成影响。练习一些精神准备的方法并且记住考试不仅仅是测试学术水平，这些方法将会减少你的焦虑感，让你在考试中有最好的发挥。

如何考试

大家都知道考试是一件十分有压力的事情，但是其实并没有想象中那么糟糕！以下是你可以完成的几件简单的事情，它们可以帮助你在任何考试中提高分数。赶快来看一下这些小窍门，并想想如何将它们应用在你的学习时间中吧。

阅读题目要求

这是最基础，但也是最容易被学生忽略而造成大量时间浪费的地方！因为阅读要求是最基础，并且可以100%防止出错的部分，我们会有专门的一部分来讲解如何阅读题目要求。

认真阅读例题。几乎所有的标准化考试都会提供例题以及相对应的正确答案。通过这些题目来确定你完全理解题目的意思，并指导如何做正确的解答。如果遇到让你困惑的题目或说明时，不要害怕去向你的导师求助。

阅读题目的技巧
对于阅读题目的技巧，我们可以写出很多很多的内容。但这里是对你最有帮助的一些。

• 先思考。在看选项之前，首先阅读和思考问题。建议你在看选项之前，先试着自己找出正确答案。这样的话，当出题人想用十分接近的答案来迷惑你的时候，你不会掉入那些陷阱。

• 判断正误。当你对题目犹豫不决的时候，可以阅读每一个选项并且判断他们是正确还是错误的。最终选择那个看上去最正确的一个。

• 标记问题。不知道为什么，很多参加考试的人不喜欢在试卷上做标记。除非有人明确告诉你不可以在试卷上做标记，否则为什么不好好利用这个机会呢。以下是更多关于这方面内容。

• 圈出关键词。当你阅读问题的时候，划出或圈出关键词。这样可以帮助你集中精神在用于解题的最重要信息上。例如，如果问题说"Which of these is not a synonym for huge?"你可以圈出"not"，"synonym"和"huge"。这样可以清除杂乱的信息，使你集中注意力到重要的信息上。以下是更多关于这方面内容。

• 一定要划出的关键词：all, none, always, never, most, best, true, false and except。

• 划掉不相关的选项。如果你被较长的题目所困扰，可以划掉任何你觉得不相关，具有明显错误，或者是你觉得用来迷惑你的信息。

• 不要试着挖掘字里行间的意思。通常来说，问题是会被直接给出的，不会有深入，或者潜在的其他意思。简单的答案通常就是正确的答案。不要过度分析！

如何考试 – 基本原则

有些测试是考察你快速抓住有效信息的能力；这类考试对于速度的要求是第一位的。其他类考试则会更侧重你对知识了解的深度，和准确度。当你拿到一份试卷的时候，仔细过目来判断一下，这份测试是在考察速度还是准确性的。如果考察的是速度，那么和其他标准化考试一样，你的策略就十分明确；在要求时间内尽可能多的正确回答问题。

但是，要注意！有一些测试是考察你是否能准确完整的回答问题。猜测答案在这类考试中是大忌，因为出题老师预期，任何平均分数线以内的学生，都能够在测试要求时间内完成考试。因此匆忙的答题并且猜测出一些不正确的答案会浪费你大量的时间！

看重每一个小细节。

如果准许你带计算器，或者其他物品进考场，一定要确保你带上它们，即时你不知道会不会在考试中用到。使用任何你可以支配的物品来提高你的分数。

与时间交朋友。

从你落笔的那一刻开始，合理的安排你的时间直到考试结束，并严格执行！事实上在标准化考试中，每一部分都是有时间限制的。考试中每一部分允许你的作答时间基本一定会出现在考试要求中，或者打印在试卷的顶端。如果由于某些原因你没有及时看到，不要浪费时间来寻找这些信息，你可以用每部分的分值和百分比来代替并做出一个有根据的时间限制推测。

根据分配好的时间对每部分进行作答，到时间后，不论你是否完成答题，都要进入下一部分的作答。严格按照分配的时间进行，你就能够完成每一部分中多数问题的回答。如果是速度测验，你有可能完不成所有的题目。不过出题老师一开始就没有希望你能完成所有的测试内容！这类考试的目的是检测你对大脑中知识的提取速度以及对于特殊信息的访问能力，这也是测试你对知识了解程度的一种方法。如果你知道你参加的考试是一项速度测试，那么你就应该利用策略争取答出最好的成绩。

轻松作答。

处理考试一个聪明的办法就是找到并先回答简单的问题。这是一个经过长时间测试后屡试不爽的方法，因为它帮助你节省的大量不必要的烦恼。首先，阅读题目并判断你是否能在一分钟之内作答。如果可以，完成题目并进行下一道题。如果不可以，先略过这一题并继续看下一个题目。当你在考试中完成对这部分第一轮的作答后，你已经回答了很多道题目。这样不仅能提升你的自信心，缓解焦虑并提升你的记忆力，你也会准确的知道剩余的答题时间，使你可以合理的分配剩余的时间。通过首先作答简单的题目来进行一下热身吧！

如果考试时间要结束了，而你没有能在计划时间内完成所有的难题，千万不要让这件事影响你。对于你来说，是否最有效的利用了考试时间，来正确回答尽可能多的问题才是重要的。因为不知道答案而没有作答所造成的失分，其实是因为你花了那些题目的时间在回答那些你知道答案的题目上。

送给智者的一句话：略过那些你一概不知的题目是一件事，但是我们不建议你略过所有你不是100%确定的题目。一个好的经验法则是，在第一次过滤时尝试着回答10个问题中的八个。

不要看你的手表。

即便在最好的情况下，参加一项重要的考试也会是一个不舒适的状态。如果你和其他人一样，你也会下意识的被分散掉手头考试的注意力。最常见的一种情况就是你会不停的看你手上的或者墙上的表。不要看你的手表！把手表摘掉放在桌角足够远的地方，这样你就不会每过两分钟就不自觉的想看一眼。最好，把手表反过来放。这样的话，每次你试图想看时间，你都能提醒自己要重新集中注意力到考试答题中。可以设定在每答完一项题目的时候可以查看一次时间。如果你觉得自己是一个在生活中动作比较慢的人，查看时间的次数可以多一些。但即便如此，也要集中精神回答问题，而不是看自上一次看表之后时间多去了多长时间。

化整为零。

当你遇到一个题目，它的困难程度甚至让你不知道题目在问什么，这个时候你应该怎么做呢？我们之前的建议是，在第一次过滤题目时你最好把这个问题略过。但是有些时候，你还是需要返回去看并解决这个题目的。这样一个让你万分焦虑并毫无头绪的题目，解决它最好的方法是把它分割成容易处理的几部分。解决小问题总是会容易一些的。对于复杂的题目来说，将他们化整为零并分而治之。一旦了解分割后的部分的内容，你就可以轻松的把小部分的内容重新组合来解决更大的问题。

从难题中找出你的解答方法。

如果你看到一道十分复杂的题目，并且你不知道如何将它进行分割，以下的这些策略可能会对你有帮助。首先，重新阅读题目并寻找提示。你能否换一种或几种方式来转述问题呢？这个方法可以为你提供一些思路。寻找到那些功能性的动词或者名词，并且将它们在句子结构中定位。请记住，英语中的很多名词都是由很多不同含义的。当中有些含义是相关的，但有的时候是截然不同的。如果当你对句子的含义不理解的时候，思考一下关键词的其他定义或意思。

事实上，想要得到正确答案，并不总是一定需要完全理解问题的含义！那些成功的学生会使用策略5，消除法，来作为答题的小窍门。大部分情况下，至少有一个答案是明显错误的，并且可以从备选的正确答案中划掉。下一步，看看剩下的选项并且删除那些部分正确的选项。可能有的时候还是需要你努力的猜测，但是使用消除法，可以尽可能的帮助你寻找到正确答案 – 即时在你不知道问题真正含义的情况下！

不要提早交卷。

即时你等不及想赶快离开考场，你也要充分使用你分配好的所有时间。相反，一旦你完成了答题，利用剩余的时间来检查你的答案。回到那些对于你来说最难的题目并检查你的答案。另一个使用这些时间的好方法是，回到那些你在答题卡上涂卡的选择题。进行抽样检查，随机检查连续的五个或六个答案，确保你的答案与答题卡上的答案相一致。这样可以检查你是否有涂错的地方，或者因为空涂一个位置而导致之后的答案都是错误的！

让自己变成一个超级侦探并寻找粗心大意犯下的错误。寻找那些含有两个否定词或者不寻常用词的问题；它们可能是用来迷惑你的。粗心的错误可能是用于你看题速度过快或者是错过关键词。例如"always"，"never"，"sometimes"，"rarely"这些词或者与它们类似的词，都强烈表明答题需要进行一些搜索来完成。千万不要因为粗心大意而丢分！

正如你在考试开始时，根据问题的难易程度安排时间的方法一样，确保你给自己留下充足的时间来检查答案。写作题目和数学题目需要你展示你的水平，检查你的字迹来确保他们是清楚可读的。

数学题目是非常需要答题技巧的。检查数学题的最好的方法是，如果有可能，使用另外一种思路再做一次。

还有一个好建议。好像不论你怎样努力和尝试，你仍然会遇到很多你不确定的问题。记住这些题目并继续完成后面的考试。如果你找不到问题的答案，可以回到试卷中并找出与同一内容相关的另一个题目，也许会给你一些线索。我们都知道参加考试是十分有压力的，并且你想尽快解脱。但是切记，在尽可能多的检查你的答案之前提前交卷，会使你更快的面临灾难。只需要花几分钟就可以使你的成绩由坏变好。更何况，在考试结束以后你会有大把的时间来放松和庆祝。

在考场中 – 你一定要做的几件事！

如果和世界上其他人一样，参加考试是你最想摆脱的事情，没有任何事情会让你改变主意。然而，即时你想也根本不可能实现。与其痛苦，不如做一些态度上的调整，也许可以将一次糟糕的经历转变成...一个不错的经历！看看以下的这些提示。通过简单改变你面对考试的态度可以改变考试经历本身。

提前进入状态。

通过几周的学习，这个重要的日子终于要来了。你可以做的是提前让自己进入考场，来体会坐在其中的沮丧，担心和焦虑。时刻检查你自己的情绪状态。如果你的情绪在考前是不稳定的，可以证明你在考试中会有一个怎样的发挥。给自己加油打气是十分重要的，要相信你自己，并且利用自信心把自己带入情绪中。

不要和现实作斗争。

大多数时候，学生都是对考试不满的，而且理由很充分。毕竟，很多人不善于考试，并且他们知道考试的成绩不能真实准确的反映出他们的知识水平。可以理解，人们对于考试不满的原因是因为，考试对学生进行划分并且创造出了看似不公平的分类制度。面对现实吧：善于死记硬背的学生而不善于内容分析的学生通常会得高分，而那些具有创造性思维并且不喜欢简单死记硬背的学生则成绩会较低。这也许是不公平的，但是现实就是这样的。遵循规则是考试的会给你加分，而创造能力则通常是减分的。对于这个现实情况来说，没有必要浪费时间和精力来懊恼。你要做的第一步就是接受现实并习惯它。当你意识到考试的重要性并且你必须全力以赴的时候，你就会取得好的成绩。想想的将来和事业，如果你能一直取得好的成绩，就会使它们更容易实现。避免那些消极的情绪并且将注意力放在那些可以提高你热情和增加你积极性的事情上。
提前到考场并给自己足够的时间放松。

如果你担忧，紧张，害怕，焦虑，或者觉得慌张，这些都会对你造成影响。提前到达考场并在进去之前放松自己。这样，当考试的时候，你就已经适应了周围的环境并且做好的考试的准备。当然，你不想太早的到考场，让自己是唯一一个坐在里面的人。那样不仅不能够帮助你放松；而只会让你有太多的时间坐在那里，又重新产生焦虑和担忧的感觉。

如果可以的话，提前几天参观一下你即将参加考试的考场。对考场有一个视觉上的概念可以对情绪上的冷静有极大的帮助，因为它带走了一个最大的"未知因素"。不仅如此，当你看过考场之后，你就会知道去考场的路线而且不会担心会迷路。而且，去过考场之后你会知道路程大概需要花多长时间。也就是说，三个潜在的焦虑因素已经被一次性的排除了。

在纸上做笔记。

提前到考场的其中一点好处就是可以给你时间来做笔记。如果你会花很多时间来担心是否能记住像姓名，日期，地点，和数学公式这些信息，有一个方法是可以解决这个问题的。除非你参加的考试允许你携带书或者笔记，（很少考试会允许这样做）否则你只能依靠记忆。提前到考场可以给你自己一点时间来开通你的记忆，并且粗略的记下一些你将会被考察到的信息点。但是你要事先确定在进入考场后是可以做笔记的；不是所有的考场都允许这样做。当你拿到试卷之后，在一张小纸上写下所有你担心会忘记的内容。只要花一两分钟把这些担心转移到纸上，就能有效的消除你大部分的焦虑和慌张。

让自己放轻松。

这里是一个可以帮助你缓解身体的紧张感，并能使你感觉舒适甚至放松的小技巧。你需要绷紧你全身的肌肉并坚持几秒钟。窍门是，你必须用力绷紧全身的肌肉才能有效果。你可能需要在家提前练习几次；毕竟你不希望在考试前由于一个不熟悉的技巧来增加你的压力感！当你达到考试地点之后，可以在洗手间或者任何安静的地点来进行这个练习。

从脸部开始，之后逐渐向整个身体过渡。绷紧，紧握肌肉并坚持一两分钟。当你向整个身体过渡时要注意每部分肌肉的感觉。扩张你的肩部来绷紧你的背部。用力吸气让你的胃部尽可能的向后面贴近，确保你的背部下方的紧张感并张开你的手指。绷紧你的腿部肌肉和小腿，然后张开你的脚部和脚趾。你整个身体现在应该和板子一样僵硬。

现在，反向从你的脚趾开始进行放松。当你逐一放松身体每个部位时，要注意每一块肌肉的感觉变化。当你放松过一块或者一组肌肉的时候，要始终保持它们放松的状态。集中注意力感受整体放松后的感觉。当放松进行到胸部位置的时候开始深呼吸。这样，在你坐在考试位置的时候，你会感受到无与伦比的放松感！

集中注意力。

少数的人可以在参加重要考试的时候全神贯注的进行作答，但是大多数人的注意力还是容易会被分散的，可能因为考场是你最不想待的地方！以下是几件可以帮助你集中注意力的事情。

远离窗户。如果你选了靠窗的位置，你可能会不自觉的注视外面的草地，而不是集中精神在考试中。而且，任何与人类相关的活动，不论是一个行人走过，还是一对夫妻的争吵或者是亲吻，都有可能拉走你的注意力而使你不能进行重要的工作。因此外面发生的任何事都不应该成为你的干扰。

选择一个远离走道的位置，当有人提早离开考场的时候不会对你造成影响。提前离开考场的人通常都是成绩不好的。千万不要和他们做时间上的比较。

当然，你爱你的朋友们；这也是他们能够成为你朋友的原因！然而，在考场中，在你的意识里他们应该完全变成陌生人。你要忘记他们的存在。要做的第一步就是坐的离你的朋友或者同学远一些。这样的话，你就不会下意识的想看看他们完成的如何，而且你们也不会有机会进行眼神的交流，既不会使你分心，又免去了作弊的嫌疑。并且，如果你的朋友或同学因为没有和你一样努力复习，他们会感到焦虑，这种感受会完全打破你平静的心理。

当然，你会希望选择一个光线好的位置。因为没有人会愿意坐在忽明忽暗或者光线不好的灯下来完成一项重要的考试。

如果外面有嘈杂的声音的话，可以请你的老师或者监考老师把门关上。如果他们不能这样做，那么就尽你最大的能力来屏蔽那些噪音。千万不要让任何事情干扰你。

确保你带了足够的铅笔，笔和任何你会需要用的物品。大多数入学考试是不允许你带任何如糖果等私人物品尽考场的。如果你要参加的考试是这样规定的话，要确保你的早餐是营养均衡的。吃一些蛋白质，复合碳水化合物和一点脂肪，来增加你的饱腹感并且提供额外的能量。没有什么是比在考试过程中突发低血糖更糟糕的事情了。

不要让温度的过冷或过热成为影响你的因素。不要考虑室外的天气状况，为了防止考场的空调开得过高或者暖气开的过低，带一件毛衣，围巾或者外套以备不时之需。处于同样的原因考虑，多穿几层衣服可以使你对气温的变化有所准备。

带着手表可以让你可以随时管理你的时间。但是对于多数学生来说，手表有可能会让他们更多的关注自完成上一题之后时间过去了多久。因此不要把手表带在手上，而是摘下来并反过来放在桌子远处的角落里。这样，你就不会因为反复的看时间而分心，而是在你需要的时候再去看时间。

喝上一加仑的咖啡或者多喝一些能量饮料看起来是一个好主意，但是事实上，这是一个非常坏的主意。咖啡因，兴奋剂或者其他人造的功能性饮料都会造成你处于一个长期兴奋和疲劳的状态。你的大脑看似在不停的运转，但极有可能它没有在正确的轨道上运转！不仅如此，饮用太多的咖啡或功能饮料会让你频繁的想去洗手间。这会耽误你大量的答题时间，并且会分散你的注意力，因为每次你离开考场时都会无法集中精神。兴奋剂只会让你在解决复杂的问题时更难的进行清楚的判断和思考。

同时，如果你正在受焦虑的困扰，尽量的避免使用镇静剂。即时是处方的镇静剂也会降低你的意识和动力。动力是你在考试的全程中都需要的。如果你由于过于焦虑而影响到你考试的能力发挥，你需要请你的医生为你开具一份医疗证明。如果有医生的证明和解释，只要条件允许，很多考试中心都会提供无干扰考场，延长考试时间或者其他相应的服务。

保持呼吸顺畅。

也许听起来很不符合常理，但是很多人在焦虑，紧张或者恐惧的情况下，他们的呼吸就会变弱，甚至有些时候会难以呼吸！要时刻注意你的情绪，当你觉得担忧时，要集中精神进行呼吸。花几秒钟来提醒你自己做规律的深呼吸。在进行稳定的吸气时，深呼吸能够为你的身体增加能量。当你持续做深呼吸的动作时，你会觉得紧张的情绪在吐气的时候被排出体外了。

在家练习呼吸是一个非常明智的方法。用这个放松式的方法进行练习，你会开始了解那些在紧张状况下紧张的肌肉。暂时称它们为"信号肌肉"。这些肌肉是你首先要解决的问题，它们需要被最先放松。花些时间来听听这些肌肉的想法并按照它们说的话去做。通过一些简单的呼吸练习，你会养成检查规律呼吸的习惯，当你意识到有紧张的情绪时，放松就会成为你身体中第二种条件反射。

考试前避免焦虑

有效的管理你的时间。

这是你成功的关键！你需要利用整块的时间来学习所有的相关材料。制作一个时间表并按照安排的时间进行，时间表可以帮助你跟踪你的进度，并且会提醒你的家人和朋友你正处于复习的紧张阶段。不论由于什么情况，你都不应该因为任何人改变你的复习安排，或者放弃学习时间去做一些娱乐活动。千万不要让任何事情影响你的学习时间！放松。

使用最适合你自己的方法来进行放松。有些人喜欢通过瑜伽来进行放松，也有些人喜欢写一些日记和随笔来表达自己的感情。有些人喜欢在地板上做仰卧起坐或平板支撑，也有些人喜欢在院子里散步进行放松。在复习过程中要适当的进行劳逸结合，放松的那部分时间也是不可忽视的。
注意饮食健康。

不要吃薯片和巧克力，而是选择新鲜的水果和蔬菜，因为它们既美味又可以帮助你提供缓解压力的营养成分。应当避免食用那些不仅不能帮你缓解压力，而是会增加压力的食物。这些食物包括人造甜味剂、糖果以及含糖类食物、碳酸饮料、薯片、巧克力、鸡蛋、油炸食品、垃圾食品、加工食品、红肉、以及其他包含防腐剂或者大量调料的食品。放弃这些食物，来一碗蓝莓和一罐酸奶吧！
保证充足的睡眠。

不要突击进行考试复习或者试着靠熬夜来完成。如果你一开始制作一个时间表，并严格按照其执行，你一定会信心满满！如果尝试在最后一分钟来突击记忆大量的信息，会导致你在第二天精神疲惫。而且，这种冲刺记忆法只会让你忘记你已经花了一周时间记住的内容。记住：要时刻提醒自己在考试当天做出最高效的发挥。

要对自己有自信！

每个参加考试的人都会感觉紧张和焦虑，但是保持一个积极的态度会缓解你的焦虑，并且使你对知识的记忆和思路更清晰。这将会是一个展示你复习成果的好机会。加油！
确保你准备好所有考试需要的物品。

根据不同的考试，你可能会允许带笔或者铅笔，计算器，字典或者草稿纸进入考场。提前把这些和你进入考场的证件一起整理好，确保考试前准备好所有你需要的物品。
不要和朋友闲聊。

要让你的朋友知道，在考场你不会和他们讲话，但这与个人原因无关！你需要找到一个远离门窗，光线好并且舒服的位置。原因是如果你的朋友担心他的紧张会给你造成压力；当然，你没有必要告诉他们。而如果你担心他们会生气，则告诉他们这可以避免他们遭受你焦虑的困扰。

常见考试错误

考试并不是一件很有意思的事情。特别是当你考试时由于一个本不应该发生的低级错误而失分，会更令人生气。那么在考试中有哪些是常见的错误呢？

忘记写名字。

你怎么能忘记在试卷上写名字呢？你可能会吃惊于自己犯这个错误的次数。经常性的，如果没有写名字，试卷会立刻被作废，考试成绩记为零。

标记错误的选择题答案。

答题的稳定速度在考试中是十分重要的，但这并不代表你要匆忙的答题。确保你写出的答案是你想写的答案。如果你在答题卡或者想圈出的答案是"C"，千万不要因为注意力不集中而答成"B"。

重复回答问题。

有些选择题有非常相近的两个选项。如果你匆忙作答，可能会选择出两个选项。切记题目只有一个正确答案，因此如果你选择了多于一个的答案，那么这道题目就自动作废。

漏答有难度的题目。

我们前面建议先略过有难度的题目，等完成简单题目后在进行作答，但是要注意！首先，确保你会回去看那些题目。用笔圈出整个题目或者在题目前面标注一个大问号，这样当你浏览试卷的时候会提示你还有漏答的题目。第二，如果你不小心跳过了题目，有可能会对你的考试造成极大的影响。想象一下，如果你遇到了一道难题，想等一下再来做。你开始阅读下一个题目，因为你知道答案所以完成了答题。当你完成了试卷的最后一题并回过头来看之前的题目却发现，你并没有跳过那道题！事实上，你把后一题的答案写在的那道题的位置上，导致之后每一道题目的答案都是错乱的！

错误的转移草稿纸上的答案。

这是一个在你匆忙答题时极有可能犯的错误！反复检查你在草稿纸上的答案，并且确认你抄写在试卷上的答案和草稿纸上的内容是一致的。

不要忽略时间，也不要被时间控制。

在限时的考试中，很多学生都因为没能掌握好时间而完不成考试。要注意控制好你的节奏！然而同时，也不要过多的关注考试的剩余时间。

想太多。

通常来说，你想到的第一个答案就是正确答案。如果你总是对自己没有把握，即时你一开始的答案是正确的，你的犹豫不决也会导致你选择出错误的答案！

准备好考试物品。

笔没有水或者没有带备用的铅笔或笔，并不能成为你考试失败的理由！提前准备好所有会用到的物品及备用物品。带上纸巾，备用橡皮，几只削好的铅笔，几节电子设备用的电池，以及其他任何你会需要用的物品。

忽略考试要求。

考试要求是十分重要的内容。如果你略读这些内容，就会很容易漏掉关键词或者曲解题目的意思。没有什么比因为没有认真阅读题目要求而考试失败更糟糕的事情了！

考试结束后：

口语考试结束后，要记得花一点时间坐下来，用笔和纸记录一下你在考试中的表现。简单记下你对自己发挥的评价以及在以后的口语考试中可以做怎样的改进。这一点对于帮助你提高未来口语考试的答题技巧是非常重要的。当你收到成绩和反馈的时候，如果你对你的成绩有任何疑问，可以联系考官和老师来寻求细节上的反馈。

免费电子书版本

请下载本出版物的免费电子书版本！
可适用于平板电脑，iPad，iPhone，或者其他智能手机。

登录
http://tinyurl.com/ycl4a9et

www.ingramcontent.com/pod-product-compliance
Lightning Source LLC
Chambersburg PA
CBHW070901080526
44589CB00013B/1155